Single Parent Superstars

Thinking BIG, Living Life & Expecting the Miraculous

-Your Guide to Transformational Parenting-

FOREWORDS

Minister Ivy Coleman, *Mentor*

To read Single Parent Superstars: Thinking BIG, Living Life & Expecting the Miraculous by Monica Thomas, is to partake of the pureness of heart and strength of character of a woman committed to God and to fulfilling the call He has placed on her life. Her passion for expanding the vision of Single Parents to do what may seem to be the impossible is a testament to her knowing that "With God...all things are Possible!"

Minister Ivy Coleman,
The Message Ministry, Inc.

Pastor Nancy Engen, *Spiritual Advisor/Friend*

Providence (I am not talking about Rhode Island) Definition: IT IS FROM GOD; from start to finish; ALPHA AND OMEGA. Rev. 1:8. NKJ

Monica and I met at an Italian restaurant in Gaithersburg, Md. It remains providential. I am not a single parent. I am honored to encourage anyone who believes in the GOD OF COMFORT (Isaiah 40:1 NKJ) to read Monica's story and ministry to others living life as a single parent.

"Our God is an awesome God! He reigns in heaven above with WISDOM, POWER and LOVE."
—Unknown

Redeemed to worship Him,
N.M.E

Ms. Rachel Ochieng, *Ministry Partner/Friend*

Quite often, the narratives of single parents present as young girls having children out of wedlock. Monica reminds us of all single parents: Mothers and Fathers, Widows and Widowers, Divorcees, the family member that steps in to care for a child. She says I see and acknowledge your struggle. This book does not dance around or deny the challenges that come with raising a child as a single parent. Through the real life stories and workbook, Monica offers wisdom, accountability and hope. The reader is encouraged to walk in Faith and Hope while developing an overcoming mindset. You walk away from reading this book empowered, knowing that God has entrusted and blessed you with the gift of a child or children you are raising.

Mr. Mac Arthur Williams Jr., ***Eldest Sibling***

Today, as I write this foreword, I share words that I always hoped I would have the opportunity to share in some shape, form or fashion. I am the older brother of the author. My experiences with her are as plain and unique in the most natural form. Being the older brother, I always took on the protective role for my little sister. One of the list of characteristics I can share is she was an exemplary younger sister, meaning she listened to all the instructions I gave her, whether out of Love or Fear. One part of my role was tutoring with schoolwork. I am renowned for the "special way" I helped siblings and close family with homework. All that I helped went on to accomplish great achievements in education. Monica was my first client. She weathered whatever I did, to get her to comprehend and understand the subject matter. I believed that to be a test she mastered. Early on Monica was able to display that she possessed servitude to move past barriers to achieve what she had set her mind to.

"Easier said than done", this book was written based on the Monica's personal experiences. What better teacher is there than life itself? I never took the time to contemplate that Single Parent Superstars actually is a destination and all that arrived there, did not travel the same road. The greatest lesson of all is that in her trials and tribulations, Monica developed an awesome relationship with Our Lord and Savior Jesus Christ. Without question, this memoir is a testimony that will lead some to travel the same road of faith. Monica has become an inspiring and affable adult.

Many thanks to persons speaking on my behalf in response
to this work, in accordance to expertise, journey, success and contribution!
-Monica

About the Author

Monica Shante Thomas

Monica S. Thomas is a widowed, single parent of two, who has had a self-described, supernatural experience as a mother. Away from her family in Georgia and on the cusp of completing her collegiate career in Washington, D.C., she quickly had to learn to navigate the new responsibilities of MOTHERHOOD as she watched her love, Carl, struggle as a black man in America, fighting demons of challenged self-worth, police brutality, incarceration, and substance abuse. Monica struggled in her new role as a single parent while trying to figure out her relationship and life as a whole, with the extreme difficulties of time spent apart from her partner. While those around her looked on in disdain and judgment, Monica ran to God and He gently came to her rescue through his WORD. Through this evolving relationship, God not only helped her, but also gave her this assignment to share with others.

Monica is now the Founder & President of Single Parent Superstars, INC, a Maryland non-profit, 501(c)3 organization, dedicated to empowering single parents – through advocacy, mentoring, and support – to be relentless caregivers, no matter the circumstance. Monica earned her Bachelor of Science from Howard University and her Masters of Business Administration from the University of Phoenix. She is currently working as a Director in the Health Sciences Department at a community college in the Washington D.C. metropolitan area.

DEAR SINGLE PARENT SUPERSTAR (SPS) LETTERS

from Monica are seated throughout book.
Be encouraged!

TABLE OF CONTENTS

SPS FOUNDER QUOTE
Trusting the Lord is a life changer.

Dear SPS Letter 1:

SETTLING IN "THE TRUTH" AND PUTTING MY CHILD FIRST

Dear Single-Parent Superstar,

One absolute truth is that a child is a gift from God, not a mistake. Now with that being said, the truth surrounding order and timing cannot be denied. When I had my first child, I was not married and in my last year of college. Was being an unwed mother in God's order for my life? Was being pregnant during my last year of undergraduate education good timing? Was my child's father in a place where he could be a good father? The answer is that even though I was blessed with a gift, the circumstances surrounding the gift were not optimal and now I was a mother, and I had a decision to make. When you have a child, whether you are the mother or father, it is no longer about you. It is ALL about the child. If you like focusing on you and not sharing the focus, the last thing you want to do is put yourself and your wants at risk by participating in things that will likely end up opposite of what you want.

The responsibility of a child is a huge, continual undertaking. It is interesting how most parents can begin to play the "blame-game". *This is his baby...he should be here!* Should he? Is he committed to you or this child? *She's always out at the club and leaving the baby with anyone who is available? She is trifling*. Is she? The best thing that a single parent can do from the start is acknowledge themselves. SPSs acknowledge ourselves. Who am I? Where am I? What happened? Why did this happen? What am I going to do now? How can I move forward in the best interest of my child first and then me? Am I going to be angry? Is there someone to blame? If so, is blaming beneficial to my child or me?

Am I going to express my anger in negative ways that negatively affect my child? Am I going to say negative things about my child's other parent while I put myself on a "soapbox"?

The truth is that no child asks to be here, and no child chooses their parents. My personal belief is that many parents don't care about their children. Please hear me out. Parents can say they care. Parents can say I love my child. However, if actions taken do not line up with love, then the truth is opposite of what is being said. "**Love is patient, love is kind. It does not envy, it does not boast, it is not proud. It does not dishonor others, it is not self-seeking, it is not easily angered, it keeps no record of wrongs. Love does not delight in destruction but rejoices with the truth. It always protects, always trusts, always hopes, always perseveres**" (1 Cor 13:4-7 New International Version [NIV]). If the other parent was irresponsible, jobless, all over the place before you conceived together and now that you've begun to focus, is it your job to do whatever it takes to make that person do better now because you're seemingly ready? Is it your job to search another person's heart and ability OR should your focus be on you and your child?

Love, Monica

Purpose

The purpose of this book is to share good news with ALL single parents. The good news is despite your circumstances, a good life, which may feel impossible to achieve in your current situation, *is* possible for you and your family. This book is my effort to share some of my real life experiences as a single parent and the Word of God to help single parents build faith and see themselves as God sees them. Historically, the position of single parent (single parent family), with all its challenges, is subpar by not measuring up to the threshold of the "standard family". This book will help single parents reset their thinking by no longer defining themselves by circumstances or societal standards. It will activate single parents into action, which is required for growth and will directly affect their children. Bad circumstances can take a toll on anyone, especially persons who have the responsibility of taking care of and rearing others.

I have had an unusual experience as a single parent. In the beginning, I was so scared. I felt the weight of responsibility and I needed help. I ran to God and submitted to learning His way through the Word of God. I was a mother, now in charge of another person's life and I figured only God could help me. With God's leading, I have experienced miracles. My experience has been supernatural. I know God expected that I would share this testimony, and that is what I have done with this work. After this reading experience, I pray single parents are encouraged and challenged to BELIEVE BIGGER and increase your faith. I pray your expectations EXPAND and you begin to SPEAK OUT what you want, not what your current situation dictates. I pray that each of you who read this book accept the following declaration, by faith, immediately:

YOU ARE A SINGLE PARENT SUPERSTAR!!!

Dedication

This book is dedicated to:

Affliction is something that causes pain or suffering. I think we can all agree that in life, we all will experience affliction. As single parents, we are uniquely positioned to experience the world with increased affliction just by the level of difficulty of our circumstances. Single Parent Superstars endeavors through curriculum, organization and all extensions to mentor, advocate and support single parents.

The Word of God says the Lord delivers His children out of ALL affliction. "The righteous person may have many troubles, but the Lord delivers him from them all"

(Psalm 34:19 NIV). Many people believe that every person is a child of God. This is not true. While we are all God's creation, each individual has a choice in accepting the gift of God through the sacrifice of the Lord, Jesus Christ, who died for the sins of the entire world. When God's creation says yes to the free gift of salvation, we then become children of God. When we say yes to Jesus, immediately we experience a spiritual rebirth and are reconciled (made right) with God – we are made righteous. We are in good standing with Him and God Almighty calls us His child. This new position is being "born again" and "in Christ".

Have you ever seen a superstar athlete perform? Superstars make things happen. They do not just accept what is happening and go along with the flow. Superstars show up and show out. In Christ, single parents have access to the demonstration of the Glory of God. Single Parent Superstars do not focus on worldly limits. We can all see the limits! That part is easy. God says "What do you want child? I AM willing, what do you believe?" God, the Great I AM, says yes!

This book is dedicated to my father, Mac A. Williams Sr. (1954-2014). He raised not only my eldest brother and I by himself, but other children had access to his person and benefited from him

greatly. He loved us. He protected us. He gave us his best, and he was far from perfect. A lot of who I am is because of who he was to me and what he showed me. He stood up for me and I learned how to stand up for mine, directly from him. He could not teach me everything but he taught me a lot.

Dedication is also to Kimberly D. Martin, the first student of the SPS curriculum, and to my children, Langston and Simone. Dedication extends to Carl, Charles, Cheyanne, and Corey who will always have a piece my heart. Thanks to Rachel Ochieng for listening ears to endless excerpts and to anyone who helped me get this assignment done.

Lord God this is my offering. I agree, obedience is better than sacrifice. "Does the Lord delight in burnt offerings and sacrifices as much as in obeying the Lord? To obey is better than sacrifice, and to heed is better than the fat of rams. (1 Samuel 15:22 NIV)

The Beginning of Revelation

Revelation is something being revealed, or disclosed.

Personal Testimony (*given at Carolina Church by SPS Founder, 2000-2001*)

Good Morning Carolina

Part 1

I have been asked to share a word with you about my experience as a single mother. My prayer in preparation of doing what was asked was that I be led by the spirit of God. The first thing I want to do is give you a little background. I was raised by my father, who had my brother (4 years my elder) and I, by himself. He was not perfect, but he loved us and was with us each and every day. When my grandmother died, we moved from New York to Georgia to live with my grandfather. I grew up in a house full of loving men. I had the love of men, and I knew what it was like to be well taken care of and protected with a stable home life. When I graduated from high school, I ended up coming to the DC metro area (D.C./Maryland/Virginia) to attend Howard University. I was not the stereotypical college student because I had to take care of myself. I worked all the way through undergrad and financial support from home was minimal. I was not angry with my daddy or my family because even though I did not have it as easy as others, according to support, I always knew that what needed to be done, could be done. When I started dealing with men away from home, I was disappointed because nobody I came into contact with, whether it be college student or local, was remotely interesting to me until I met my son's dad in 1995. My interest question was answered by him. The bottom line is that we were young. On one hand, there he was, young, smart-dumb, wild, despaired, and rebellious. On the other hand, there I was, young, smart-dumb, unlearned, with no knowledge of life outside of my protected box. Our son Langston was born in February 1998. I had one year left of undergrad and Langston's dad was on a serious downward spiral. Not only did he already have three children he had not gotten a handle on supporting, but now he had another child on the way. Two months after Langston was born, his dad was incarcerated. NOW WHAT? RIGHT!

Part 2

At that moment – in that place and time – I was in shock. I was experiencing something serious that I had never seen or heard of before. In that time, I became available to God. My heart was available and so was my mind. For some reason I was not scared. I guess I wasn't smart enough to know that I had good reason to be scared. Thinking of that time, I remember my house being warm. The atmosphere was thick, warm and comforting. I had never felt the presence of the Lord by myself like I did during that time. I knew that Jesus was there. I could reach over and touch Jesus in my house. I was comforted. Somehow, I began to do all that I had to do immediately for myself and for my son.

Part 3

I've heard people give testimonies and acknowledge how Pastor Moore (Anthony Moore/ Carolina Church), was the father they never had. Well, that was not my testimony. I had a father. My acknowledgment to my Pastor is that he ignited in me a thirst for the Word of God at a time when I was available to hear. Not in a hearing only way, but in a hearing and submitting kind of way. Pastor Moore was like a glass of water and I was a slice of bread...just absorbing everything he was preaching and teaching...JUST LIKE GOD INTENDED FOR ME. I began to learn about life. I began to receive wisdom that was from God.

Part 4

The next few years were a struggle. I thank God for allowing me to see that the struggle was mine and everything I was experiencing was a result of the choices I had made. It was not Langston's dad's fault. Neither was it my dad's fault. You know how a lot of women believe that when they get pregnant, the whole world is supposed to flip upside down. That man who had no job before she got pregnant is supposed to be putting out resumes now, right?! That man who was irresponsible before she got pregnant is supposed to be picking up his cross and running now that she just delivered that newborn, right?! WRONG! God says, "**My people are destroyed for lack of knowledge.**" (Hosea 4:6 King James Version [KJV])

Unfortunately, single motherhood can be compared to having a disease. I would not wish it on my worst enemy. The best thing about it for me is the little piece of heaven God placed in my hands despite of myself. Now I know people do not like to say or hear that, but it is the truth. When I see a single mom functioning in that capacity, I feel like dying inside because I know first-hand how hard it is in so many different ways. I will tell anyone who will listen about my struggle, in hope they will embrace victory in Jesus. It is totally un-natural to get up, get your child to school, go to work, take calls from school at work, work all day, get off, get your child, do homework with the child, cook dinner, and do not try to pursue your education and have your own schoolwork to do, and at some point, settle down with no hug or kiss form your husband and then get prepared to do exactly the same thing the next day.

Now here is the build-up...

Single mom...single parent...Monica...you can do it. You can do all things through Christ who strengthens you. It is not easy, and it is not what God intended, BUT it can be done. If it is too hard for you to do it well...then you should die trying...WHY??? Because you are worth it. Your child is worth it. God has already made the provision...you just have to tap in. Tap into acknowledging where you are. Tap into processing how you got there. Tap into receiving and submitting to the wisdom of God. After you have tapped in, of course you will still have struggles, but it is nice to know that I might have fainted by now, or even died, if I were not confident of this one thing – I WILL SEE THE GOODNESS OF THE LORD IN THE LAND OF THE LIVING.

I have experienced miracles already. God is still teaching me and I will see the goodness of the Lord in the land of the living.

GLORY TO GOD. HE IS MY ONLY HELP. HE IS ALWAYS THE SAME. HE LOVES ME UNCONDITIONALLY AND HE WILL NEVER, EVER LEAVE ME ALONE!

-testimony end

The Assignment
"HUMBLE BEGINNINGS"

So where did the serve single parents assignment come from? How did the effort form? Well, I'm glad you asked. I remember it like it was yesterday. After my son was born, my life changed. Since I was pregnant during my last year of undergraduate at Howard University, finishing college was a tall feat. Truly, the Lord made a way out of no way. I had the feeling that I had to work in the "real world" now. I have this kid. I have to get a real job. I have to start working now at a new level. It is funny when I think about it because I always had a job. I worked throughout college and had real bills like rent and utilities alongside my best-friend whose parents paid her portion. I learned early on that looking to the left and right at others has nothing to do with me, so I pressed. I landed my first real job (benefits, opportunities etc.) at a genetic research organization in Rockville, Maryland. That is what got me into MO County (Montgomery County, Maryland). I was a college graduate. I was a single parent. Moreover, I was a new member of the corporate America workforce, which is a whole different book! My family was in Georgia. My son's dad was struggling with life and incarcerated, and I was a brand-new mom with the largest responsibility that I had ever had on my hands – someone else's life.

Now let us backtrack just a little here. I got saved at age 13. In the Bible, John 3:16 says, "God sent his only begotten son, so that whoever would believe in Him, would not perish, but have everlasting life." Saved means that you have accepted the FREE gift of salvation. Saved means that you have received forgiveness of sin by the grace of God. You are justified or redeemed to Father, God. You are in right relationship with God. It means you confess Jesus as Lord and Savior. It means you have eternal life in Christ Jesus.

Growing up, my father would drop my brother and I off at Sunday school but didn't attend himself. If he came inside with us, he would leave as soon as the singing was over before the preacher started. LOL! I remember feeling like I was not alone as a child – like someone was with me, walking alongside me. Now that I am older and have learned a few things, I have words to describe it, but I remember it, God's presence, just as plain as day. As a college student, well before I was pregnant, I was drawn to the local church. Something pulled me. It was likely what I had experienced as a child and surely the leading of the Holy Spirit, even though I could not articulate it at that time. I visited many churches that where in my reach during college because I got something in that environment that did not exist elsewhere at that time. I heard the good news of the gospel and accepted the Lord Jesus early in my life. Even as I was filled – immediately – with the Holy Spirt, I had to live, grow and am still living and growing even until this day. So, when I walked into premarital sex and pregnancy out of wedlock and just not having a clue about life at all, I was still a child of God. At the point of single motherhood in my life, I had hit a very low, low. I was functional and moving but I was aware that I needed help. I had a child now and I needed BIG help. I ran to my heavenly Father.

This is where it gets interesting because I really, really did run to the Lord. I had reached a level of submission where I was seeking after the Word of God and being in His presence, like I had never before. I had always been aware of Him, but now I was nestling myself in His bosom. I needed help. I needed guidance and confidence. I needed something that I just could not get from other human beings. I have this child now! I thought...*I am not perfect Lord, I know. The whole world is looking at me thinking I am the stupidest person alive; I know.* I honestly did not care about what they thought, I didn't have time to care. *I am somebody's mama now* became my stance. *The people who really love me are not here, they are in Georgia. The man who loves me and this child, is in jail. Lord help me.* So, I took a deep dive into whatever was available through my local church. Sunday service, bible study, classes...God's presence!!! *Now*, I understand that there is liberty in the presence of the Lord. *Now*, I understand that when I am weak, He is strong. *Now*, I understand that even before I knew what I was doing, the Lord was leading and guiding me. *Now*, I understand that He is truly how I live and move and have my being. I am His child. I remember God responding to me continually. It was truly just me and Him. He not only gave me strength and revelation for my very desperate single parent situation, He also downloaded a whole lot more single parenting information and insights that had absolutely nothing to do with me, relatively speaking. The downloaded information was much bigger than just my life, it was for you too. He opened my eyes and heart to what single parenting was and must be. He began to show me things with such depth, and I paid attention and learned. I became so aware of single parents everywhere. It was too much! I can honestly admit I wanted to turn it off. But it was on now! God began to give me wisdom and knowledge and grow me in a way. Since He stretched my view and gave me a depth of insight and compassion with more and more information that was bigger, smarter, and more lovely than me, it became clear to me that He had given me an assignment. I had to share, that is what He wanted. There was purpose even in my desperate situation. He was helping me and preparing me to serve others. This is how Humble Beginnings (Single Parent Superstars) was birthed!

Humble Beginnings to Single Parent Superstars

As I evolved as a child of God, as a person, as a mother, so did the framing of the assignment. I initially called the organization My Sister's Keeper. It is funny how, I was raised by a single father, but still minimized single parenting to women, solely, though it was my father who raised me after my parents divorced. Now that I was a single mom, for some strange reason, I associated my status with women only. I learned that was a limited perspective. At another point, the organization was called Humble Beginnings. Even still, one day I got a revelation. There is no humble beginning in Christ Jesus! Even when we get saved, eternal life, light, freedom is instantaneous! We go from darkness into His marvelous light. We go from being the walking dead into living forever! We do not get a little saved, we say yes to Jesus and it is done! I wasn't a little bit of mother. I was a MOTHER all the way live! I was immediately committed, immediately focused, immediately energized...I had the gift of a child. I had someone's life in my hands. The name Single Parent Superstars is a state of mind. It is an elevated status. It is what I am and you are, by Faith. I am a Single Parent Superstar. You are a Single Parent Superstar. Every day we do our best because we love our children. Do we dot every "I" or cross every "T"? No! However, we can do all things through Christ who strengthens us. It is not about what I can do, it is about what God will do through me! There is unmeasurable benefit for my child and me and He, God, gets the glory in my being a single parent superstar, not me! Through faith, the impossible becomes possible. This is what God showed me and where the name Single Parent Superstars was confirmed.

WHAT *exactly* is a "SINGLE PARENT SUPERSTAR?"

A single parent superstar is a single parent who does their very best every day to positively affect their kids. No parent is perfect, but single parent superstars work with purpose, putting their children first at all times. Life has proven to present difficult circumstances. Single parent superstars are a community of parents who strive to overcome the difficulties of life for themselves and for the benefit of their children. When people hear single parent superstars, they automatically think of a single parent who makes lots of money or who have highly educated, high profile kids. They think of single parents who may own property or properties. They think of single parents with minimal struggle, if that exist at all. They think of what the world deems as good success and somehow that must be what a single parent superstar is. That is NOT what a single parent superstar is. Material things (cash, cribs, cars, access etc.) do not make single parent superstars. We can have cash, cribs and cars and be killing our kids at the same time, or causing them to want to kill themselves.

"My daughter is a lawyer or doctor because of my hard work" or "All my kids graduated college because I didn't let anything stop me!". I have heard many single parents who have "beat the odds", self-righteously, speak that way about their children – essentially taking all the credit. Sure, they have a right to be proud. However, we never hear anyone bragging about his or her children's pain, suffering or failures. You never hear single parents taking credit for when their children do not quite meet society's standard of good success.

There is much reference to children honoring parents. I am sure you've heard people quoting Exodus 20:12 NIV, "Honor your father and your mother, so that you may live long in the land the Lord your God is giving you". But we hardly hear the same folks or anyone for that matter quoting Colossians 3:21 NIV, "Fathers, do not embitter your children, or they will become discouraged". The Oxford Dictionary defines embitter as *angry or resentful at having been treated unfairly; to excite bitter feelings; to make bitter*. Single parent superstars strive to give life to children, not take it away. We want them to keep heart, not lose it. There is hope and a future in Christ Jesus no matter what circumstances exist. In a single parent superstar's home HEALING is the children's bread. Whatever is needed to promote healing, is what single parent superstars look for.

In an effort to help clarify real meaning, here are a few situational examples of single parent superstars that people do not usually recognize:

- If I am a 30-year-old single mother, addicted to drugs with 4 children, and somehow, in a moment of clarity realize my children are neglected or suffering due to my condition and I decide to ask one of my siblings to please take my children for a while, to help them, I am a single parent superstar. This is a single parent superstar move.
- If I am a 24-year-old single father with 2 daughters and I decide not to entertain random women in front of my daughters, this is a single parent superstar move.
- If I am gainfully employed with a horrible boss, who makes my days at work more challenging than they need to be and I choose to respect authority in my best effort to maintain my job, for the good of my family, this is a single parent superstar move.
- If I am a 46-year-old single parent who enjoys "rachet" music, but I decide to only listen to it when I am alone and not engage while in the presence of my children, this is a single parent superstar move.

Common themes in the examples above are sacrifice, consideration, introspection, thoughtfulness, humbleness, long-suffering, and ongoing service to children over self. These are all single parent superstar qualities.

Single parent superstars recognize our circumstance is not optimal, but are relentless in our dedication to not settling or giving up. Single parent superstars acknowledge difficulty and recognize we need help. We need God to help us do what seems impossible. A single parent superstar keeps hope alive and expects that somehow, they will make it because they walk by faith and not by sight. We have too much at stake to just throw in the towel. I have to tell you, if you ask me how I got over or how I get over, I will tell you my truth. My truth is that the Lord helps me. My truth is that while no one in the physical is to my left or right, I am not alone. I run to God and have learned how to operate in that capacity because I do not have any other options that are hundred proof. I need results. My children need results. God is the same yesterday, today and forever. He is Faithful. There may be persons who reject the good news of the gospel of Jesus. I hope that is not you but if it is, feel free to use everything else provided here and I wish you well. But, if you ask me how I made it or make it, I must credit God. I cannot do anything well without His supernatural leading.

Wouldn't it be great if every day single parents were just perfect? That is not reality. We all need God, His Word, His Way, each and every day of our lives. No one loves us or knows us better than Him. The Bible tells us "...do not be conformed to this world, but be transformed by the renewing of our minds, that you may prove what is that good and acceptable and perfect will of God" (Romans 12:2 New King James Version [NKJV]). God is telling us to not change ourselves to be like the people of the world or not to let the world define us, but to let Him change us from the inside out, with a new being, a new way of thinking. Then we will be able to understand and see what God wants for us in our single parent situations. We will understand more and more about what is possible through us, with His power. We will be able to know what is good and pleasing to Him and what is perfect for us and our kids. He loves us. If God wants it, it is to our benefit. We will be able to understand what is possible in Christ and the power we have as children of God. How can we lose with the stuff we use? I mean if God is for us, who can be against us? God loves us unconditionally and wants us to know it. God is on our side and wants us to know it. God loves our children more than we ever could and has purpose for them in this world. In our care for the children, we are simply helping them meet their purpose. God is not punishing us in our single parent status. He has not turned his back on us and left us destitute. This is what people make God up to be in their minds but this is not the personality of God at all.

Consider this, the world says that single parents are less than or last. God says that we are more than conquerors in Christ Jesus. The world says our children do not have a real family and are subject to not being fully protected and cared for. God says I will provide all of your needs according to My riches in glory by Christ Jesus. The world says single parent families cannot withstand what is necessary to produce productive children who are well-adjusted and emotionally stable. God says we are like Him, and we overcome the difficulties of the world by faith in Christ. He says we can do ALL things through Christ who strengthens us. Knowing, believing, speaking and walking out what God says about us is ongoing. It doesn't just happen one day and then we are good forever. Faith comes by hearing and hearing by the Word of God. No Word, no faith. No faith, no confidence to move. No growth, children suffer. Single parent superstars take the power posture, as we are presented with situations daily that affect our children's lives and work to make good choices continually. We choose life continually. This is not a moral thing; it is a position thing and even a power thing. The supernatural power of God gives us the ability to do the impossible. Because of Him, we are blessed, empowered to prosper. We are not alone. God gives single parent superstars confidence to go over and beyond and to expect His goodness and mercy. The declaration of being Single Parent Superstars is made by faith. Our faith activates us and effects our realities. What we believe effects our children's lives.

I heard a very smart, seasoned woman use the word *wayward* one day. I understood the context of the word to some degree but, I was so intrigued by it, and its usage, I looked it up to gain understanding. Wayward is defined as **given to or marked by willful, often perverse deviation from what is desired, expected, or required in order to gratify one's own impulses or inclinations; Resistant to guidance**

or discipline; "Mary Mary quite contrary"; "an obstinate child with a violent temper"; "a perverse mood"; "wayward behavior". (Definition.org)

Whoa! That is a direct, no nonsense, comprehensive explanation of what it means to be wayward men and women or much worst, PARENTS! There is no perfect parent and there is no perfect child. But, 'what we ain't goin do' is willfully throw our children under the bus or turn a blind eye and pretend we do not have a clue.

Single Parents Superstars are the opposite of wayward. We are single parent superstars when we dedicate everything we do in support of the positive-growth and development of our child(ren). We are not willfully rejecting what is required to raise our children. We do not reject guidance or discipline. We do not display violence toward our children. We are not just trying to be. We are relentless caregivers of our children, no matter what circumstance we find ourselves in. We are today, right now, SINGLE PARENT SUPERSTARS! That is our declaration in Jesus' Mighty Name.

Now, it should be crystal clear what a Single Parent Superstar is.

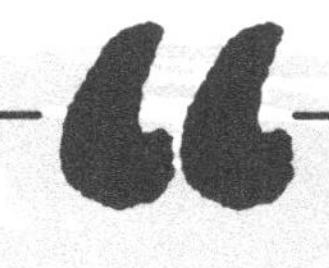

SPS FOUNDER QUOTE

God makes the impossible possible in my life.

Dear SPS Letter 2:

HOME LIFE "THE GUARDED SANCTUARY"

Dear Single-Parent Superstar,

I remember when my son was about 2 years old. I lived in a garden style, yellow brick apartment complex at the corner of North Capital and Missouri Avenue in Northwest, DC. My son and I lived alone in this apartment for a couple years. I saw other people who lived in my same building and complex, for that matter, going about their lives. I have always had in my heart the urge to engage on some level and share the love of God. There were a group of teenagers I had seen many times, who lived in the community, and we would speak whenever we crossed paths. One day, one of the guys from that group had his afro out, and we began discussing cornrows when he mentioned that he didn't have anyone to braid his hair. I said, "Oh, I can do it for you!" So we agreed on a date and time and the "community service" outreach was set. When the scheduled evening came, the young guy showed up at my apartment and I welcomed him in. I was seated on the couch and the guy was sitting on the floor in-between my knees as I began to braid his hair. As I worked through, I noticed that his hair had not been washed and there were dandruff flakes. I was honestly grossed out but committed to doing what I said I would do for the young fella. I had done about four to five braids and was halfway done when up comes my son, serious as a heart attack and says, "Alright mommy, that's enough!" My son wanted dude to get out...and to get out now. Evidently, it had been building up in his little heart because by the time he came over I heard the forcefulness in his voice. I could tell that he was being affected by what was going on. I think I remember telling my son that I was almost done to get him to back up and chill out. As I continued braiding and chatting with the young man and I finally asked him,

"How old are you anyway?"

"Thirty-something."

"OH MY GOODNESS, let me hurry up. You're older than me!

My son was right – you got to go!"

I finished braiding the grown man's hair and he thanked me and left. I'm pretty sure I washed my hands like 10 times in some type of pine sol/ water solution. LOL!!!!

Now that is a funny memory, but I have to say that I will never forget how my child was affected by this person in my house. The guy wasn't loud, rude or doing anything to make anyone uncomfortable. However, the fact of the matter is that my son's attention, focus, comfortability was affected. Let's think about this for a moment. Let's say it is a school night and you've gotten home with your children. It is time to relax, do homework, and get dinner started. What is the focus of your home in the evening? What is your focus on a school night? Is your child comfortable? Have you provided a decent spot for them to sit and do homework? Are strangers or familiar distractions there? Do you have company? Is the TV on music videos, reality shows or anything distracting while little Johnny or Sarah are doing their homework? What is the environment like for your kid(s)? What are they seeing? What are they hearing? How is today similar to yesterday and how will it affect tomorrow?

I can honestly say that I observed my son being much more than what meets the eye. He wasn't just a little two-year-old, unaware of his environment, void of emotion or opinion. Furthermore, he felt the need to protect what was his. He felt the need to protect his mommy, his home – his environment. My son is not an island. I submit to you that all children are grossly affected by their environment. It is our job as parents to do our best to provide an environment – continually – conducive to positive growth and development. It doesn't have to be a huge house or even totally isolated. What it has to be is intentional. Single Parent Superstar can anyone come to your house at any time and do anything they want? As parents, we have to ask ourselves is it about me or is it about my kid?

I have another story to share and this one includes a loved one, so I'll be discreet. I remember it being a beautiful Saturday afternoon. I had finished up an early appointment and decided to stop by this person's house to see her children. I did not call first, I just stopped by since I was nearby. I knocked on the door and when she came to let me in the kids were nowhere in sight, and she had company, four guys sitting in the living room in folding chairs. They were probably neighborhood guys she knew and from what I could tell they were just chillin' on a beautiful Saturday afternoon in her apartment. She told me that the kids were in the back. I walked to the room and found the kids in a bedroom gathered in a corner playing on the floor. They were not dressed. They were just in that room, quietly keeping each other company. I want to say here that I am not judging this loved one. I did that day, but I'm not now. I was alarmed that she had a bunch of dudes in her sanctuary. They were in her family's sanctuary, had taken over, and she was A-Okay with it. The children were not even a factor as far as I could tell because she was disconnected from what they were doing and just chillin' out with the dudes in front of her TV with 40s. *If you don't know what a 40 is…google it.* I was angry. I did not have the right to be angry, but I was. It was a very sad scene. I was bothered that the kids weren't doing something, anything, that involved them or even perhaps outside playing. When I left, I cried because I love the kids and I had no control or influence over what their day to day lives were like. Heck, I had my own life going on with my own mess. This was many years ago and I will never forget what I saw, the thoughts that I had, nor how I felt.

But guess what…it wasn't about me. It wasn't really about her either, it was about the children. Is home a safe sanctuary, where the children are number one? What are they seeing? What are they hearing? How is the parent showing them love? How are they feeling about themselves? What messages are being communicated to them about who they are and where they stand? I have learned that what we see and how we feel can take us on a trip. Mama's choices are affecting the kids. Daddy's choices, Grandma's choices, whoever is in their sanctuary. Anything does not go. Interestingly enough, we still have the audacity to expect them to go to school and do well. *I'll be wayward but I love you and I'm going to just hope that regardless of what I choose to do, you'll be okay*. Now, don't get it twisted…there are many children who are in horrible environments and somehow exceed expectations. This is a fact. Moreover, there are kids who have great environments and still go to the left. Single parent superstars are not in absolute control of outcomes. We are in control of intentions and choices. We have put our children first so that no matter the outcome, we've done our best. We did not allow anything to go on and we protected our sanctuary.

YOU ARE A SINGLE PARENT SUPERSTAR!!!

Love, Monica

Single Parent Superstars (SPS) Organization/ Culture: Serving Single Parents

How can I serve single parents? How can I mentor, advocate for and support them? Through establishing the Single Parent Superstar entity/ organization and pushing the culture through with a vision, mission, faith principles, motto and a curriculum. That is how.

SPS VISION

Single Parent Superstars are parents who do their very best every day to positively affect their kids. While no parent is perfect, Single Parent Superstars work with purpose, putting the children first at all times. Life has proven to present difficult circumstances. The Single Parent Superstars vision is to act as a community of parents who, through advocacy, mentoring and support, strive to overcome the difficulties of life for themselves and for the benefit of their children. SPS also provides a pathway to international travel for single parent families. Together, we lift our thinking, pick up our children and travel the world!

SPS MISSION

The Single Parent Superstars mission is to empower single parents, through advocacy, mentoring and support, to be relentless caregivers, guiding their children's positive-growth and development, no matter the circumstance. SPS also provides a pathway to international travel for single parent families.

SPS FAITH PRINCIPLES:

Proverbs 23:7 KJV
As a man thinks in his heart, so is he.

James 2:26 KJV
Faith without works is dead.

SPS MOTTO

Together, we lift our thinking, pick up our children and travel the world!

Single Parent Superstars
"Traveling the World"

SPS Motto: Together, we lift our thinking, pick up our children and travel the world! Isn't this book about supporting single parents? What in the world are you talking about picking up our children and travelling the world? That seems to come out of left field! Well, please allow me to explain. That portion of the Single Parent Superstar revelation was the very last piece of this puzzle and this is how it happened.

Part 1

I was over forty years of age, had experienced going from baby mama to wife to widow, and paid more bills than the law should allow but I had never, ever left the country. I would always think, *I am over forty and have never left the country.* I was familiar with the hustle and grind of daily life. I was familiar with responsibility and sacrifice, and it was not a priority for me to just plan an international trip. It just didn't make logical sense. During this time my son was a middle school student at Robert Frost Middle School in Rockville, Maryland. Two of the greatest leaders and protectors of children I've ever met were Principals at this school, Dr. Jones and Mr. Johnson. I remember at the end of touring the school with Dr. Jones, he told me, while standing in the front office, that the school had a sister school in China and that Robert Frost 7th and 8th graders had the opportunity to go to China as exchange students for ten days! Immediately, when I heard this, I said, "I want my son to go. I want Langston to go!" At that time, I worked at the Venter Institute on Shady Grove Road in Rockville. I was a Science Education Leader on the molecular biology lab bus. My co-workers were Darryl (the bus driver) and Crystal. Crystal was the Lead Science Educator for the program. I will not lie. I don't remember exactly which one of us, Crystal or me, came up with the idea, but we decided to raise the money for Langston's trip to China on Facebook. I was not social media savvy so Crystal led the charge in setting up the fundraising engine. The fundraising goal for the trip was about $2,500. Now, that is not a whole lot of money, but it was money that I would never have just been able to simply pay out of my monthly budget. I was not rolling like that in my new widow role with two children, daycare, rent and on and on. But I heard something good. An opportunity had presented itself. The Principal shared information about an international traveling opportunity that Frost students had access to. I heard something! I heard what he said and I did not count my son out. I wanted the something! I wanted my son to take advantage of this opportunity that had presented itself. I did not think about limits in that moment. I did not cancel my son or my family out. I did not stick to practical thinking or settle for what made sense. I'll admit, I was "thirsty". I had already experienced not traveling internationally and I was approaching my 40s. I wanted my child to go further faster than me, even though I was a new widow with a new baby in a very desperate state. I wanted this and something in me propelled me to make a faith move. Crystal and I posted the fundraising engine on Facebook and the money started rolling in. Five dollars here, ten dollars there, twenty dollars over there, fifty dollars from there! There was a deadline and friends, family and strangers were participating in one way or another with the effort. The night before the deadline, we were about $500 short of the goal. I was mentally exhausted. I spoke with Crystal before I went to bed and decided to wash my hands of it. Meanwhile, Crystal, a smart phone, group chatting fanatic, was not asleep. She was awake and in a virtual group chat with people she was only a little familiar with. She just couldn't rest until we had all the funds.

That morning, Crystal called me and asked had I checked the fundraising engine to see if we had met the goal. I was like uh...no. She strongly urged me to look as she began explaining what happened after we spoke. "I was in a group chat at about 1A.M. with people I don't know personally. In the middle of the conversation I asked if there was anyone who wanted to help my friend's kid go to China?" There was a stranger on the chat who responded and asked how much was needed. I gave the lady the amount and she told me she would add the funds to the engine right away". As I listened, I got online, looked on Facebook and low and behold, all of the cash had been collected! While I was sleeping, God was moving. He had a stranger give my friend all the money that was needed for us to reach the China goal. He used my friend, in her group chat, to say something that moved a complete stranger to provide what was needed. It was done. I had done all I could and came up short. God came in and finished it *with the largest donation at the very end from a complete stranger on a group chat*. LOL! Langston was going to China for ten days as an exchange student with Robert Frost Middle School. I was 40 years old and did not have a passport yet, but now my son would. I was struggling and my husband was deceased, but our son was about to go on his first international trip. It was a miracle!

Part 2

Fast forward to 2018-2019 and Langston became determined to study abroad at some point while in college. During his junior year, he fulfilled that desire by studying abroad in Ecuador. I was 45 years old and decided not only did I want to go visit him in Ecuador before he completed his full year, but I would also take my daughter, Simone. So here I am a widowed, 40-something mother of two and I was only just now preparing to get my passport. Not only was I going to take my first international trip but my daughter, who was only 11 years old at the time, was getting her passport and preparing to have her first international traveling experience. LOL... look at the Lord God! I began to do things to make space for this in my mind, in my schedule, and in my budget. Simone and I took the passport photos, and I got the applications submitted. One day, I received two packages in the mailbox. I opened one and there was my passport. I was thrilled. I had always said, *I am over forty and have never left the country*, yet now I was holding my passport in my hand. Then as I opened the second package, which felt a little different, it contained a letter stating that Simone's passport could not be issued because additional forms were needed to prove her father was deceased. I was so angry and disappointed. If that was needed, I could have already have done all this. I was so put off. Grudgingly, over the next few weeks I sent the additional forms to the office. On another random day, Simone and I went to the mailbox and there was a familiar looking package there. I was like oh my...this must be it. I grabbed all the mail and we proceeded in the house. When I got upstairs, I remember Simone sitting in the kitchen at the table. I opened the package and it was her passport. I was so excited. I said, "Simone it is your passport. Simone, you have a passport. Simone you are only 11 and you have a passport!" Simone was not paying me any attention at all. She replied, "Okay Ma. I know Ma. Yes Mama, it is a passport." LOL! Can you believe that. We were having two totally different experiences. Anyway, I thought to myself, I'm over forty and have never left the country, yet now my son has left multiple times and my daughter will experience international travel way before me and my son. Look at God! Now watch this. I went to bed floating on cloud nine because Simone had her passport, and we were going to Ecuador in April. The night came and went. The next morning when I arose, I was still floating. I floated right in the restroom and got a Word from God. I was floating and getting revelation at the same time. God made it clear to me that the Single Parent Superstars organization would fund single parent families traveling abroad! This is why I was still floating. I was having a supernatural experience with God. Really Lord?!?!?!! This was the portion that was the most miraculous. This was the portion where God would do for us what we couldn't see space for or what we could not do for ourselves. This is the portion where the impossible simply becomes possible. This is the fun. This is the extension of love just because He is God. Yes, SPS mentors, advocates, and supports but through it there is an extension of love from God. This is a "trip by God". Single parents do not have the responsibility of paying. God pays and does so through the vehicle of Single Parent

Superstars INC. Imagine God saying, "Here you go! Go do something fun, that you may not see space for now and by the way, it is on me, the Lord God!" That is where the international piece came from. Not at all from me, but from the Lord.

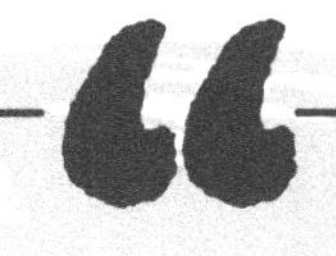

SPS FOUNDER QUOTE

When people counted me out and left me to die, God came and recused me.

Dear SPS Letter 3:

LIVING A LIFE BEFORE A CHILD

Dear Single-Parent Superstar,

Children are so smart. They are like little sponges. They see things. They hear things. They have feelings. I'd even say they are underdeveloped adults. Okay, maybe that is a bit much. They are formed miraculously in mommy's womb. They are organisms having an experience with their environment from the very beginning. I would imagine mommy's belly is a good place to start, warm and cozy with all their needs being met. I wonder when they begin to hear things. I remember my husband talking to our son when I was pregnant. We weren't married then. I also remember him talking to our daughter when I was pregnant. He died four days before our daughter was born. Since she has never seen him with her eyes, I wonder if she heard his voice when she was in my belly. Long before I was pregnant with my daughter, I remember planning to name her Mya, but when I was actually about to have a daughter and had to really confirm her name, Carl did not agree. He never, ever called her Mya. One day we talked about it and settled on a new name, Simone. I do believe that as she heard Simone over and over again, she became a "Simone". Now that she is here and I've experienced her for some years, she is definitely a Simone. I hope that Simone heard our conversations and somehow found comfort in hearing her dad's voice, since she never got to see his face or feel his touch.

SPS consider their children at all times. Everything we say and do affects our child's growth and development. I have said things like "actions speak louder than words" and heard others say things like "I can show you better than I can tell you". Both of these statements ring true. However, in the case of raising children, it is about show and tell. As a parent, I am continually speaking and doing. I am responsible for managing their experience to the best of my ability because I have charge of their lives for a time. There may be times when I do not have absolute control but for the most part, my handling will be a leading force in what they experience from day to day. Who is the adult in the situation? The parent is. Who is the leader and the guiding force in the situation? The parent is. Who are the children watching and listening to day in and day out? The parent is the answer! That level of influence if far reaching. It is not inconsequential and will affect generations to come.

One thing that I have learned is that it is impossible to please people. No matter what, there will always be someone who thinks that you missed the mark or someone who thinks that all of your decisions are bad. As I've matured, I've become better and better at taking the good from people and leaving the rest with them. As adults, most of us really don't care what other people think and this is not a bad stance. However, we should always care about what our children see and hear as well as the environment they experience which will impact their growth and development. It is interesting how no matter what they experience, they will grow and develop, whether it be positive or negative, there will be an outcome. There is no formula to parenting. No parent is perfect and children are not perfect. Nobody is perfect. We need God to parent children. As Single Parent Superstars, we do our best daily and we need the leading of the Holy Spirit. Parenting is not an automatic transmission. It is a stick shift. Okay, that joke may have failed but you get the point.

Love, Monica

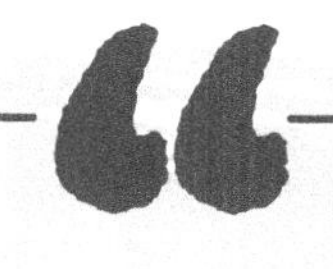

SPS FOUNDER QUOTE

God loves our children more than we do!
He wants them and us to reach for the stars!
We can trust Him. He is willing and able!

SPS Curriculum

Everything good and perfect in my life comes from the Lord. The SPS Curriculum is God inspired, consisting of a group of faith-based Principles and Misconceptions. Oxford Languages dictionary defines a principle as *a fundamental truth or proposition that serves as the foundation for a system of belief or behavior or for a chain of reasoning*. It defines a misconception as *a view or opinion that is incorrect, based on faulty thinking or understanding*. The notion of a Single Parent Superstar by faith is a base. Who am I? What do I have the ability to do? How can I do what is necessary?

Shortly after my husband died and the heavy support from well-intentioned people dissipated, God came and told me He was the Lord my God who will take me by the right hand. He told me not to fear, I will help you. This word I got from God gave me peace during a severe storm and propelled me forward, day by day. The SPS curriculum comes from the same space. He is the Lord our God who holds us up with His righteous right hand and tells us, don't live in fear, I am your help. This word, this base, will speak to your heart and change your mind. It is built to give you and your children a hope and a future. Single parent, if God be for you, who can be against you? He is the same yesterday, today and forever and makes the seemingly impossible possible in our lives. Now, if you reject that notion, and say, "Monica I don't want your Jesus. I am not a believer and I get sick of hearing about that repeatedly", my response is okay– please finish the book and try to consider the SPS curriculum and attempt to apply the principles and misconceptions to your life. I really hope and pray there will be some benefit for you, no matter what your current thinking is. I still declare by faith, YOU ARE A SINGLE PARENT SUPERSTAR and I pray God's best for you. I can only tell you my truth, share my experience and do what I have been told to.

Single parents, I suggest after reading each principle and misconception to pause for just a moment to consider your response. I encourage you to write your responses down, no matter what they are. There is journaling space called THINK RESPONSE, for you to right down exactly what comes to mind. Remember the SPS Motto: *Together we lift our thinking, pick up our children and travel the world*.

Let it rip!

Single Parent Superstars "PRINCIPLES"

SPS Principle 1

SPS are fearless and do not allow fear to paralyze us. We do not give up or make decisions that would hold our children back.

#Relentless Caregivers

THINK RESPONSE

SPS Principle 2

SPS have self-control; they choose not to respond with emotion that would negatively affect their children. They understand their kid(s) are watching and modeling behaviors perpetuated in their environment.

THINK RESPONSE

SPS Principle 3

SPS understand that children are gifts from God, not punishment.

THINK RESPONSE

SPS Principle 4

SPS learn from past mistakes. We forgive ourselves and work hard not to repeat actions that have yielded undesired results.

#Acknowledgement Is A Starting Point

THINK RESPONSE

SPS Principle 5

SPS are not jealous of their children and can accept when other safe, well-intended adults take interest in them, providing opportunities or support that may be out of the parent's reach at the moment. SPS understand that seeds of positive growth and development planted in their children can come from others and benefit not only their child(ren), but also the rest of the world.

THINK RESPONSE

SPS Principle 6

SPS understand that home is a protected, safe place for their children no matter what home is. They don't allow external elements to overwhelm the home they've made for their children.

THINK RESPONSE

SPS Principle 7

SPS are visible in the children's schools and in the community. We can be seen! We do not hide out and leave our children to whatever the world offers. We are involved and engaged, which can happen at different levels, depending on life's requirements. We do not ever think the little we may have to offer is nothing or not worth it. We find a way to offer whatever we have. We get our "hands dirty" supporting our children and the benefit is circular in that other families are doing the same.

THINK RESPONSE

SPS Principle 8

SPS are accountable. They do not sit, aimlessly doing nothing and just hoping their children will be okay. Every action they make is in support of the positive growth and development of their children.

THINK RESPONSE

SPS Principle 9

SPS do not speak negatively about their children's other parent. They understand that blaming is a waste of time and effort. They realize that the other parent, no matter who they are or what they do, are part of who a child is.

THINK RESPONSE ______________________________

____

____

____

____

____

____

____

SPS Principle 10

SPS understand that it is not our job to trust. We watch, pray and ask questions. We do not turn a blind eye and leave our children to family, friends or strangers. Is it really a good idea to allow our children to spend the night with adults just because they have extended niceties towards our family? Who are you and what is your interest in my child?

#It Is Not Our Job To Trust!

THINK RESPONSE ______________________________

____

____

____

____

____

SPS Principle 11

SPS speak life to our children. We call our kids what we want them to be. We understand that life and death are in the power of the tongue. SPS create their future with our words. We know our words go straight to the heart of our children.

#Lift And Subdue

THINK RESPONSE

SPS Principle 12

Women SPS understand their sons are NOT their man. Men SPS understand their daughters are NOT their woman.

#Healthy Relationships With Children

#Kids Are Not Partner Fill-ins

THINK RESPONSE

SPS Principle 13

SPS dream! We set goals (write them down and make the vision plain) and we plan to achieve them. We are the first inspiration for our children.

#As A Man Thinks In His Heart, So Is He.

THINK RESPONSE

SPS Principle 14

SPS understand that help and support are nice, but nobody owes us anything! We forgive persons who refuse to give support and accept that ONLY God will withhold nothing good from us. When we see properly, we understand that He is our source.

#God Is My Source

#We Cannot Beat God's Giving, No Matter How Hard We Try

THINK RESPONSE

SPS Principle 15

SPS do not pretend. We know actions of overcompensating or over-indulging will not fill voids of pain, disappointment or shame for us, nor our children. SPS overcome difficulties by believing and moving forward one day at a time. We do not give up.

#The Lord Is With Us Always and He Promised to Never Leave Us Alone

#Faith Is Action

THINK RESPONSE

SPS Principle 16

Where will our children's identities and esteem come from? Will it come from television, social media or other agenda-based expressions of this dark world? Will we be so engrossed into how we want to recreate as adults, and dismiss the listening ears our children? Who will be the parent? Who will exercise boundaries and self-control? Who will set limitations? How can SPS listen to music with explicit lyrics in their children's presence and expect them to go to school and have interest in reading, mathematics or art? We are what we eat! How can SPS have potty mouths with vicious speech and expect the children not to be exactly the same and worse? They cannot! SPS choose life daily. SPS pay attention and care about what influences our children. We monitor what goes into their eyes and ears until they are able to do it themselves. Our children are growing continuously and must be able to make good choices on their own. When and if we choose to recreate with adult rated entertainment, we do so on our time. We will not do it at the risk of negatively affecting our children's positive growth and development.

> Train up a child in the way he should go, and when he is old, he will not depart from it. – (Proverbs 22:6 KJV)

#Our Children Are What They Eat.

THINK RESPONSE ______________________________

____

____

____

____

____

____

____

SPS Principle 17

SPS are not selfish. We are not willing to put the notion of a new love interest over the immediate needs of our children. Children suffer from the pains of divorce, loss, loneliness and rejection too. SPS support their kid's healing opposed to diving into temporary fixes that can have far-reaching consequences.

#New Love Is Timely and Healthy. Anything Doesn't Go

#I Have Nothing to Prove

#I Am Good Enough

THINK RESPONSE

SPS Principle 18

SPS Pray! We open our mouths and offer continual thanks to the Lord. We praise Him for our many blessings. We remind Him of His promises to us, His children, and we declare not only what we need but also what we WANT!

Lord You said if I acknowledge You in all my ways that You would direct my path. – (reference ([ref.] Proverbs 3:6)

I am strong and courageous. You told me not to be afraid of anyone or the difficulties of life. I am not alone because You said you would never leave me or forsake me. - (ref. Deuteronomy 31:6)

SPS, the only thing we have to fear is fear itself. We must speak the WORD!

Come boldly to the throne of grace to get mercy and grace in your time of need. – (ref. Hebrews 4:16)

THINK RESPONSE

____

____

SPS Principle 19

SPS cook! Home cooking is more affordable, healthier and presents teaching opportunities from one generation to the next. Eating out is expensive and lends to overeating, weight gain and more. We do enjoy outside food sometimes, however SPS work to maintain a healthy balance. Fast food is high is saturated fats and calories. It is "real" food but a low grade eating option. All of us would benefit from considering nutritional value labels, which provide a healthy dose of reality (calories per serving, number of servings, salt, sugar, etc.). If we are not careful, we and our children will balloon right in front of our eyes. I know it takes time to shop, thaw, cook, repeat, repeatedly. Our lives are so busy and sometimes pulling over to McDonald's seems like it makes sense. But does it make sense 3-4 times a week? I am talking to myself with my Chic fil A issues. Nothing beats a home cooked meal. Let's give our children's bodies a chance to be healthy and strong. Let's cook more than anything else! Bon Appetit!

#This Is Deep Right

THINK RESPONSE ____

____

____

____

____

____

____

____

SPS Principle 20

SPS overcome the difficulties of circumstances by FAITH in Christ. SPS strive to love daily, regardless of how they feel or what they see. We have children to raise and they deserve our best effort!

#SPS Are Perpetual Overcomers

What Is Love?

Love is patient, love is kind. It does not envy, it does not boast, it is not proud. It does not dishonor others, it is not self-seeking, it is not easily angered, it keeps no record of wrongs.

Love does not delight in evil but rejoices with the truth. It always protects, always trusts, always hopes, always perseveres.

Love never fails. – (1 Corinthians 13:4-8 NIV)

THINK RESPONSE

SPS Principle 21

SPS communicate preventative measures to anyone who will listen, especially the closest ones to their hearts (children they influence, close friends, love ones etc.)!

#LoveSpeaks

- Abstinence is not an enemy.
- Our bodies should be reserved for our husband or wife.
- Sex should not be therapy.
- Just because my or others choices were not optimal, doesn't mean better choices for you are impossible.

Fact: If it is easy, or the whole world is doing it, it is likely the wrong thing to do and that is real talk.

And you will know the truth, and the truth will set you free. – (John 8:32 New Living Translation [NLT])

My people suffer because of a lack of knowledge. – (ref. Hosea 4:6)

SPS communicate hope and truth, and we move forward. Be encouraged!

Together we lift our thinking, pick up our children and travel the world.

THINK RESPONSE

SPS Principle 22

SPS work to not fail at self-love and care. Even though we are charged with an unimaginable amount of continuous work and responsibility, we are committed to developing habits that promote good health and wellness.

We take walks.
We jump up and down.
We drink water.
We eat fruits and vegetables.
We laugh.

We do not accept a big "F" in self-love and care.

#I Matter Too

#I Will Never Give Up

> I can do all things through Christ who strengthens me.
> – (Philippians 4:13 NKJV)

THINK RESPONSE ____

____

____

____

____

____

____

____

Single Parent Superstars
"MISCONCEPTIONS"

SPS Misconception 1: "I don't have a real family".

#The devil is a lie

> Then you will know the truth, and the truth will set you free. – (John 8:32 NIV)

I struggled with this misconception, especially after my husband passed. I always felt that what I had – family wise – wasn't enough. I remember feeling like I needed to be somewhere else and with others. I felt my home was empty and nothing was really going on. At some point I realized that this was a lie! I want you to know that your family is real. I am still learning how to enjoy my own space with my children – building what is fun for us – using whatever resources are available. It can be done, and I believe we get better and better at it. Be encouraged!

THINK RESPONSE

SPS Misconception 2: "My baby is a mistake".

#The devil is a lie

> They hear my voice and the voice of the stranger they do not follow. – (ref. John 10:5)

The Lord is the giver of life, and every person is unique with God-given purpose. SPS must acknowledge that their circumstances are, likely, not optimal and because of that, result in a more difficult experience, in one form or another. The difficult circumstance does not remove the fact that life is God-given, and that new life is a gift, full of love and purpose.

This is where our ability to show love is a must, even as we see or feel the "sky falling". The child did not ask to be here and deserves not to suffer at the hand of an angry, depressed, or neglectful parent.

A GIFT is a thing given willingly to someone without payment. When I think of God giving me a gift, I cannot help but imagine the beautiful possibilities that are wrapped up in it! We need to act like we know until we really do know!!!

SPS have freely received, and we freely give. – (ref. Matthew 10:8)

THINK RESPONSE

SPS Misconception 3:

"I did not make this child alone. It should be 50/50 support between mother and father."

#The devil is a lie

#I will not live in denial

> I can do ALL things through Christ who strengthens me. – (Philippians 4:13 NKJV)

All children have a mother and father. Unmarried parents must focus on themselves, not the other parent. SPS give 150%. We do not stand and wait, only doing half of what is necessary, expecting nor demanding the other parent live up to OUR expectations. Each parent should go over and beyond. A truer picture of ratio is 150:150.

Now if one parent has it "together" or seems to be working harder than the other for the child, it is not their job to be on a parenting soap box or to become the other parent's Holy Spirit (God).

It takes two to tango and the job of a single parent is hard. It is not hard because the other parent sucks – it is just hard. SPS cannot overcome by thinking the world's way. Emotional responses to life's issues do not help our children. SPS make their children the #1priority, NOT the other parent who is not their spouse.

If My people who are called by My name will humble themselves, and pray and seek My face, and turn from their wicked ways, then I will hear from heaven, and I will forgive their sin and heal their land. – (2 Chronicles 7:14 NKJV)

SPS, God loves us unconditionally and causes us to prosper! Be encouraged.

THINK RESPONSE

SPS Misconception 4: "Because we had this baby together, you belong to me."

#The devil is a lie

#negative

> For I know the plans I have for you," declares the LORD, "plans to prosper you and not to harm you, plans to give you hope and a future. – (Jeremiah 29:11 NIV)

This misconception haunts many of us, even if we are unwilling to admit it. It doesn't just matter what we say, it matters what we do. Actions speak louder than words.

- When two unwed people have a child, there is no contract, no agreement, no undertaking, no guarantee, no pledge, no promise, no bond --------- not between each other. Now responsible adults should support their decision to bring a child into the world. Most often, two adults find it very difficult to be on the same page, as it relates to a child they both love when there is no official commitment. It is not impossible, but it has been proven to be continually very difficult.
- Just because we were intimate together and produced a life does not mean we belong to each other. Children are not glue.
- As individuals, we belong to the Lord, if we believe and receive Him in our hearts. God will make beauty from our ashes. (See Isaiah 61:3 at the end)
- The Lord is the only one who will never, ever, ever leave us alone. We must learn to seek Him and trust Him.
- Raising a child is a big deal and when we acknowledge the Lord, He directs our path. Important things can be done at a certain level when drawing from His strength and direction, not our own. None of us are perfect, but growth and adjustment should be the response to pain and suffering, not choosing more pain and suffering.

- Having multiple children with a person does not make them ours and does not equal agreement.
- Having babies with different people and/or children in multiple households does not equal an easy way.

Peace---gone

Money---gone

Children---confused

New relationships---compromised

SPS overcome and there is no place that we cannot rebound from in Christ. Our commitment to ourselves and our child(ren) with the right focus equals moving forward. Old things have passed away and all things are made new with the Lord. The possibilities are endless.

Mended hearts---ours

Kindness---ours

Love---ours

Peace---ours

Provide for those who grieve in Zion – to bestow on them a crown of beauty instead of ashes, the oil of joy instead of mourning, and a garment of praise instead of a spirit of despair. They will be called oaks of righteousness, a planting of the Lord for the display of his splendor. – (Isaiah 61:3 NIV)

SPS God has a hope and a future for us! Be encouraged.

THINK RESPONSE

SPS Misconception 5: "God is punishing me."

#The devil is a lie.

#God is on OUR side!

> Every good and perfect gift comes from the Lord. – (ref. James 1:17)

This misconception is one that many single parents struggle with. Let me begin by reminding you that God loves us. Jesus was sent by The Father for every human being, which includes single parents. His blood sacrifice covered the sins of the world.

He paid the ultimate price which demonstrated His great love for us. All we have to do is believe and receive Him.

God is NOT sitting in heaven, mad at us, thinking of how to hurt or withhold goodness from us. He promised to never withhold any good thing from us. (ref. Psalms 84:11)

Raising a child is not easy. God has blessed us with children, so why would He turn His back in our time of need? The truth and good news is that He wants only good for each of us and actually causes us to prosper. He tells us to come boldly to the throne of grace to obtain mercy and grace in our time of need!

I have experienced very difficult things in my life and I'm almost certain you have too. I'm not naive nor in denial about the difficulties of life. I have learned what my position in Christ is a child of God. I understand that there is nothing I can do to separate myself from His love. I did not earn it. He freely gave it and we can freely receive it.

When bad things happen, understand that we live in a fallen world and we struggle with flesh and humanity. We do have an enemy who wants us to die in sin. However, in Christ we have the victory over sin, death and shame. Through the free gift of salvation, God saves us and promises to never leave us or forsake us.

The enemy accuses us by saying things like:

You messed up and now you deserve to suffer.

You're stupid.

Nobody loves you.

Your life doesn't have purpose.

You can't raise this child alone.

You can't help anybody.

You don't have a chance at a good life and never will.

The devil is a liar and he would like to paralyze us with fear. But the Lord, Jesus intercedes for us! Jesus perfects our prayers and God Almighty hears us. We create with our words.

God says:

I died so you can live and be free.

I love you unconditionally.

I forgive you.

I am your protector.

Ask me for wisdom and I'll give it to you freely.

I supply ALL your needs.

I deliver you from ALL afflictions.

No weapon formed against you will prosper.

You are made new in Me. Old things have passed away.

Thank you Lord!

Parenting, in general, is challenging. Single parenting is even more challenging. But I know God is my help and I can do all things through Christ who strengthens me, and I want you to know it too! No matter the circumstance, I believe what God says and I expect His goodness and declare His WORD over my life and the lives of my children, and you should too! I WILL SEE THE GOODNESS OF THE LORD IN THE LAND OF THE LIVING, and you will too!

The enemy is a liar and has no authority over the children of God. Sometimes we mess up and bring difficulty on ourselves and blame others. Lord help us. But guess what...it is okay to make a mistake and there is NO condemnation in Christ Jesus. He wants us to have good life now and in eternity with Him. We are forgiven! God is not punishing us!

> Then you will know the truth, and the truth will set you free. – (John 8:32 NIV)

SPS God is love. Be encouraged!

THINK RESPONSE

SPS Misconception 6: "God is ignoring me."

#The devil is a lie!

Be strong and courageous. Do not be afraid or terrified because of them, for the Lord your God goes with you. He will never fail you nor abandon you. – (ref. Deuteronomy 31:6)

Many SPS struggle with this misconception. Sometimes things seem so hard, and we feel as if nobody cares – not even God. I remember feeling that I know God cares, but I just don't understand why things are so hard for me or why, since God loves me, He is allowing me to experiene this continuous distress. My circumstance were horrible. I recall challenges in every part of life. I had financial challenges, workforce challenges, family challenges and within it all, my child was the priority. There were challenges everywhere and I did not just have myself to care for, I had a kid that I had brought into the world. I recall in my early 20s realizing how mean and selfish the world was, yet the only thing I had that was true and dependable was the Lord. I won't lie, I have experienced lowly times, but God was always there. I remember situations being at very low points and the devil, our enemy, would try to make it even worse. But the Lord God protected me.

After my husband died, I received many comforting cards. There was one in particular that after reading it, I realized God was speaking to me. It read:

I am the Lord thy God who will take you by the right hand and tell you do not fear... I will help you.

This WORD comforted me amid the shock and pain. This WORD came alive for me instantly and lives on in my heart to this very day, years later. The truth is that the Lord knows the plans He has for us. Plans to prosper us and not to harm us, plans to give us hope and a future. – (Jeremiah 29:11 NIV)

The truth of the matter is that God rescues us. WE ARE NEVER ALONE OR BEING IGNORED!

- We may be in fear but...

  God has not given us a spirit of fear, but of power and of love and of a sound mind – (2 Timothy 1:7 NKJV)

- We may be in ignorance (lack of knowledge) ...

  My people suffer for lack of knowledge. Because you have rejected knowledge, I also reject you as my priest; because you have ignored the law of your God, I also will ignore your children. – (ref. Hosea 4:6)

- We may be in rebellion, anger or unforgiveness...

Let us come boldly to the throne of grace, that we may obtain mercy and grace in our time of need. – (ref. Hebrews 4:16)

Fear, ignorance, rebellion, anger, unforgiveness, none of these are from God.

God never ignores us. God loves us today and every day! He loves us with a fierce love! For while we were yet sinners, Christ died for us. God's love is perfect and unconditional.

SPS let's open our hearts and mouths and lift up the Name of Jesus! Thank the Lord for who He is and what He has done! If you feel like you're being ignored, tell Him you want a closer walk –a more intimate personal relationship with Him. He is there and He will respond.

God loves us too much to create us and ignore us. He wants us to believe and freely receive the free gift of salvation. We cannot earn the love we receive from Him! We just have to accept it.

SPS God is not ignoring us! Be encouraged.

THINK RESPONSE

SPS Misconception 7: "I am alone, and I cannot raise my child on my own."

#The devil is a lie!

> I can do ALL things through Christ who strengthens me – (Philippians 4:13 NKJV)

Alone is defined as having no one else present or being by oneself; on one's own. Therefore, if the goal is to identify limitations, to go by only how we feel or what we see and leave it at that, then we can simply say I am alone. However, if victory is the goal, it is not beneficial to ourselves or our children to identify limitations and declare defeat by saying, "*I cannot do this!*" or "*I don't have what it takes to work hard like this continually*", it is actually accepting defeat.

There is life and death in the power of the tongue. – (ref. Proverbs 18:21)

SPS we must choose AND speak life. I'm declaring that we are not alone because the Lord promised to never leave us or fail us. – (ref. Deuteronomy 31:6)

Our spiritual reality is higher than what we see and how we feel. Most of us don't realize our words have power and the ability to create reality. We must change our minds and hearts and speak the truth, not our feelings. If we cannot do this, then who will?

- Daily, who will love my child by action?
- Daily, who will speak kind words to my child?
- Daily, who will model positive behavior and forward movement for my child?
- How is my child to learn that all things are possible if not by watching me?
- Who is my child to trust and have hope in?
- Who will teach my child not to be fearful, but to be powerful, show love and think about things properly if not me?

SPS our mindset is we must do this, and we will not give up. We are worth it and so are our children!

Moreover, if we want to build relationships and community, we must show ourselves friendly. We are not islands and there are friends who can become closer than family. What we want from others we should try to BE for others. I recently heard a great woman say, "If you ain't giving then you ain't living!"

SPS we are not defeated. If God is for us, who can be against us? – (ref. Romans 8:31)

Since He did not spare even his own Son – Jesus, but gave him up for all of humanity won't He also give us everything else? – (ref. Romans 8:32)

Who shall separate us from the love of Christ? Shall trouble or hardship or persecution or famine or nakedness or danger or sword? – (Romans 8:35 NIV)

We are more than conquerors through Christ Jesus! – (ref. Romans 8:37)

Neither height nor depth, nor anything else in all creation, will be able to separate us [SPS – *emphasis added*] from the love of God that is in Christ Jesus our Lord. – (Romans 8:39 NIV)

SPS we are never alone! We can do this and much more!

Be encouraged! We are SINGLE PARENT SUPERSTARS!!!

THINK RESPONSE

SPS Misconception 8: "Asking for help is a sign of weakness."

#The devil is a lie!

> Ask and it will be given to you; seek and you will find; knock and the door will be opened to you. – (Matthew 7:7 NIV)

There is no reward for suffering in silence and allowing our children to suffer along with us. Some of us think that God is watching and saying, "Okay, I've made them suffer long enough. Let me fix it now", as if the Lord is playing a game with us. This is faulty thinking and FALSE!

> The Lord delivers His children out of ALL affliction. – (ref. Psalm 34:19)

Others of us think the devil is watching us and hoping that he will be like "Okay, let me let up a little bit. I really don't want them to die." This is also faulty thinking and FALSE!

The enemy really does want all humankind to die! Period.

SPS, we cannot settle for an uninformed form of godliness, making up how "we think" the Lord operates. If we have accepted Jesus as Lord and Savior, we are His children.

> So if you sinful people know how to give good gifts to your children, how much more will your heavenly Father give good gifts to those who ask Him. – (Matthew 7:11 NLT)

If we have not accepted Jesus as Lord and Savior, we can, in a moment's time, thank Him for dying for our sins and ask Him to come live on the inside of us and to fill us with His Holy Spirit....and it is done! This is forreal.

The Lord is sun and shield! He gives grace and glory and will NEVER withhold any good thing from us. – (ref. Psalms 84:11 [emphasis added])

Asking for help is not weak! The Lord tells us to come boldly to the throne of grace to obtain mercy and grace! Silent suffering is pride, fear, and shame. All of these things are flesh and the Bible says there is NO GOOD THING ABOUT THE FLESH. No, not one! SPS daily work to put our children above these negative emotions.

If our minds are governed by flesh, it leads to death. When we govern our minds by spirit, we have life and peace. – (ref. Romans 8:6)

Help can come from different sources and in different forms. SPS don't reject help. We watch and pray. We are observant and teachable. We don't kick away good information or practices. We learn from others. We seek after persons or situations that challenge us, not persons or situations that only comfort or make us feel good. This approach does not support our growth. I recently heard a very smart woman say, "I don't turn down nothing, but my collar!". I've applied this to my life, and I encourage you to do the same.

SPS let us open our mouths and say: *Lord help me be willing to take advantage of every resource you make available to me, especially other people!* The wealth of the wicked is laid up for the righteous and our heavenly Father owns cattle on a thousand hills! We must believe what the WORD says, speak the WORD and expect what the WORD says to come to pass!

SPS let us work to live lives of giving in as many ways as possible, no matter how we feel or what circumstances look like. Giving is more than just about money. We can give in whatever capacity we are able to.

Give, and you will receive. Your gift will return to you in full – pressed down, shaken together to make room for more, running over, and poured into your lap. The amount you give will determine the amount you get back. – (Luke 6:38 NLT)

SPS ask for help! We understand that as long as the world remains, seedtime and harvest will not cease.

Be not deceived, God is not mocked; for whatever a man sows, that he will also reap. – (Galatians 6:7 NKJV)

SPS we are not weak! Be encouraged...

THINK RESPONSE

SPS Misconception 9: "My salary is nice. There is NO need for my child's other parent. We good!"

#The devil is a lie!

> Fathers, do not irritate or exasperate your children [with demands that are unreasonable, humiliating or abusive; nor by favoritism or indifference. Treat them tenderly with loving kindness], so they do not loose heart and become discouraged or unmotivated [with their spirits broken]. - Colossians 3:21 (Amplified Bible)

If we are honest, we will admit it is unreasonable to pretend that our children only have one parent, **us**. Why in the world would a person choose to make a baby with another person and then turn around and decide the child doesn't need the other parent? Is arrogance, selfishness so strong that we allow ourselves to ignore or dismiss a child's WHOLE OTHER SIDE OF A FAMILY?! Yes, of course it is!

Yes, relationships can go left, and circumstances can be kind of horrible, but those things are unavoidable and tough decisions have to be made. However, if it is just because my ex has a new "bae" and I'm feeling some kinda way about their relationship and I determine "we" don't want or need him/her.... that type of thinking can lead to frustrating a child in the long run.

"I got my good government job, a house, a car and my salary is on point. My baby don't want for anything. I can give my child whatever he/she needs."

UNTIL YOU CAN'T! Until that child begins crying out for the missing piece of their heart. Until that child is doing whatever it takes to fill the black hole in their heart.

SPS's money is good and necessary, but it and other material things cannot substitute for a child's other parent or the whole other side of a family. Positive connections exist outside of our family. Even if the other parent is questionable, it doesn't mean discard the whole family.

The child did not choose to be here and did not choose either of their parents. Mature adults, focused on making a not-so-great situation good, are willing to reach out and connect with the other side in any positive way possible – for the **child's** benefit.

My adult feelings don't matter because I'm grown. SPS are not selfish or arrogant. We are teachable and willing, especially when it benefits our children.

We don't want our ignorance or selfishness to frustrate our children.

We don't want our limitations to choke out our children.

We want our children to breathe.

This world is hard enough on its own and to make matters worse, to be in the care of a parent who thinks money will fix a child's mind and heart or who thinks about themselves more than the child – an innocent, impressionable, gift from God – makes things worst.

SPS it is never too late. Pride is an enemy. The Bible says in Proverbs 16:18 that pride comes before a fall. I do not want my pride to make me fall or cause suffering for the very thing I claim to love more than anything else in the world. Let's exercise power over pride. This is possible! Flesh and feelings cannot be how we engage. The spirit of God on the inside of us strengthens and helps us to do what must be done. We got this. Be encouraged!

THINK RESPONSE

SPS Misconception 10: "Sacrifice has an end."

#The devil is a lie.

> For even the Son of Man [Jesus] did not come to be served, but to serve, and to give his life as a ransom for many [the whole world]. – (Matthew 20:28 NLT [emphasis added])

Some single parents struggle with accepting that once we have children, they become the number one priority. All of us struggle with it at some point! The longer we take to accept this basic truth, the more difficult time we have. Agreement with the Lord is good, even when it does not seem easy. Agreement and acceptance of truth helps us to make progress.

> Agree with God, and be at peace. – (Job 22:21 English Standard Version [ESV])

One morning on the way to school, my daughter began to question me about the day their father (my husband) died. She had real questions in an instant. I know that children long for both parents no matter what circumstances have taken place. Her questions showed me in yet another way that she thinks about this and at that moment, wanted to talk about it. We talked for a few minutes and then she went to school. Within minutes, I got a call from the school counselor saying that she was crying and upset about thinking about her father. I spoke with Simone and she was able to go on with her day. At some point later that day, I spoke with my BFF (best friend forever) who was very concerned about me. I appreciated her concern because I am a person too, however, I communicated to her that my focus was not on me, but on my kid. Admittedly, my heart and even my body reacted to what I had experienced that morning. However, my priority was how I could help my daughter.

I remember watching and attempting to help my oldest child cope with the grief of their father dying. I did and do my best and pray that it is good enough but I don't know absolutely. Now that I am watching my youngest struggle. What if I thought *I've already done this! I'm tired of this. What about me? I have sacrificed so long and now I'm done and need time for me without the level of giving that may be required. She is just going to have to find a way to work through this...my other kid found a way. This is not fair...why me?* LOL...yes I laughed at those sentiments. They are not sound thoughts. They are destructive, paralyzing thoughts.

These are the facts...

We love our children, by action, daily.

We want them to live and not die and to declare the works of the Lord – (ref. Psalm 118:17)

There is a cost to laziness, disregard and ignorance.

We cannot live comfortably knowing that our children are suffering, and we have no response.

Those are facts! I tell myself *if they see me try and draw strength day by day, then they will know to try and draw strength day by day.*

SPS, the joy of the Lord is our strength. (ref. Nehemiah 8:10) We trust in the Lord and expect deliverance out of all difficulty. (ref. Psalm 34:19) That is what He promised His children in His WORD. God is not a liar! The Lord is how we live and move and have our being. We are not alone. God loves our children more than we do and because they are here, we know they have purpose.

What do we believe? Do we believe that we will see the goodness of the Lord in the land of the living? Are we just waiting for this single parent thing to end? Are we just wanting to die? Are we committed to declaring the Word of God no matter what we see or how we feel? We must! Our children are much too valuable for us to close our eyes to them.

I believe there is great reward when we sacrifice and attempt to do our best. There are rewards all over the place and the Lord does more for us than we can think or ask. Sacrifice is worth the effort. Moreover, Almighty God is putting us first SPS...all the time, causing us to prosper! Isn't that good to know? We are his favorite child!

Faith comes by hearing and hearing by the Word of God. Get a Word to stand on!

So the last shall be first, and the first last; for many be called, but few chosen – (Matthew 20:16 KJV)

SPS sacrifice has no end! We can do all things through Christ who strengthens us!

Be encouraged!

THINK RESPONSE

SPS FOUNDER QUOTE

Faith ain't free but it is money in the bank.
We cannot fake faith or buy faith.
We can only build faith and it works!

Dear SPS Letter 4:

WRESTLE TO REST (MENTAL/ EMOTIONAL/SPIRITUAL)

Dear Single-Parent Superstar,

How do we deal with watching our children – the very persons we love more than anything in the world – suffer? Yes, we have learned how to work at levels where we do more before 9am every day, repeatedly, than others do all day because there is no other choice. Daily, we prioritize our children first, which requires doing whatever it takes! And, for the most part, we get it done. WE DO IT, no matter what ***it*** is. What about the times when even that level of commitment falls short? Have you ever been willing to give your right arm if it meant, "fixing it"? I have. I have been willing to give an arm and a leg, but no matter what I was willing to do in a particular situation where I was watching my kid suffer, it fell short. I will be transparent and confess, as my son came into manhood, alone, and did what he could to manage the stresses of being without his father, racism and discrimination at school, isolation in a "community", and then coming home to me...whew chile. I was the one he was left with. I laugh now but trust me, it was far from funny. I saw what appeared to be hate in his eyes when he looked at me. I know you are likely asking, "What did you do?" My response to him was not confrontational. It could have been though, right?! My posture could have been to check my son because I was the one who was there, providing a roof over his head. I was the one working full time, shopping for and feeding that dude and his sister. I was the one killing myself to stay afloat with a smile. *How dare you look at me with hate in your eyes? You'd better fix your face!* No...nope that was not my response. My response was quiet. I continued to love my son consistently with motherly, parental actions. I could see how he felt in his eyes though. No matter what I did, I could see the suffering. It ripped my heart out. I continued to love even as some nights I would go to bed and cry for hours until I fell asleep. Honestly, I felt anger at times. I had thoughts like *whatever, I can only do what I can do. If you want to die, I will not be able to stop you*. Please do not be alarmed at my thoughts. Feelings and emotions can take you on a trip. The flesh is stupid and I do not like words like stupid. God told me after my husband died, that He was the Lord my God who takes me by the right hand, and tells me do not fear, I will help you. My actual response to my kid was to focus on God and to serve my son. I did not look to my son for warm, fuzzy thank you moms. I did not look to him for I appreciate you mom with big hugs. I did not even look to him for smiles and comfort. I settled that I would look to the Lord for all those things. The Lord would be pleased with my sacrifice and the He would gratify me. The Lord would pat me on the back. The Lord would see, care and comfort me, kiss me and encourage me. I am telling you the truth; this was my posture. I know it was the Holy Spirit leading me. What did my son owe me? Nothing. LOL. My kids did not ask to be in this world. My son did not ask his father to pass away, to be fatherless. He didn't ask to feel the pain of the world on his shoulders without the person who would initially offer him comfort and identity. He didn't ask for teachers to look at him and despise him for no reason at all. My kid did not ask for the hole in his heart. Neither one of my kids asked for that. How can I as a parent expect or require them to comfort me? My kids are not my God! The Lord, God Almighty is my refuge and my fortress! He is the One who sees and knows all, and is willing and able to FIX IT – not my kids! It will take time. It will take order. It will take the leading of the spirit of God to meet individualized child needs, but He is able. He is faithful. We must wrestle to rest when we witness our children suffering. We do all we can do but we must take it to the Lord in prayer. Give it to Him. We must keep our eyes above the waves in the Name of Jesus! Not only can He fix it, He will fix it. It is already done! We walk it out by faith and trust in God. We are diligent in our commitment to our children and then ourselves.

YOU ARE A SINGLE PARENT SUPERSTAR!!! Be encouraged.

Love, Monica

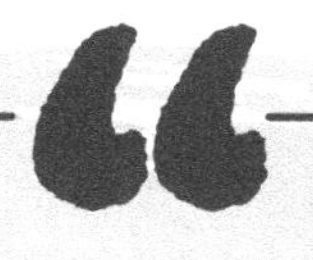

SPS FOUNDER QUOTE

If I am telling the truth, I am giving God all the Praise because He did it. He does it. If it is good, it is God! He does it for me, He will do it for you.

Dear SPS Letter 5:

ENCOURAGEMENT TO REST (PHYSICAL)

Dear Single-Parent Superstars,

I would like to encourage you regarding RESTING.

I've struggled in this area. Since I've had to do a lot – most of the time – on my own, I've realized that I didn't really know how to just do nothing and chill without guilt. I've had to rediscover how I like to have fun. I encourage you to, when the opportunity presents itself, take a breath!

The Lord has energized me supernaturally because I asked Him to. I needed His help to do things at a certain level *and* keep my sanity. The daily grind of home, work, kids and community can be overwhelming. He is whatever we need and I am thankful for that. SPS let's remember to ask Him for what we need and want and believe He provides!

Yes, we are thankful for all we have the opportunity to be a part of! Yet, don't forget to do something for ourselves like take a walk alone, read a book, or go see a friend who we haven't seen in a while. Do something different and light...even with the kids.

Take a few minutes and chill the freak out, then get back to it! When we rest, it is GOOD for us, and everyone around us benefits, especially the kids.

#Sit down and clear your mind
#Ress (not rest)
#Peace and discovery OR rediscovery
Be encouraged!

Love, Monica

SPS HIGHLIGHT STORIES

SPS June 2018 HIGHLIGHT Story of the Month
MIKKA NEWSOME is a SINGLE PARENT SUPERSTAR!!!

Mikka is a 38-year old mother with a 19-year old son. Her sister, Bobi Newsome, passed away 5 years ago, leaving two surviving children, ages 4 and 15. Mikka has the awesome assignment of raising her niece and nephew as her own children.

Anyone observing Mikka sees her daily sacrifice and commitment to each of her children. She is selfless, dedicated, and consistent with a joy that shines bright for the world to see. Mikka is a beautiful woman with a witty sense of humor that is infectious.

I asked Mikka to share something with other SPS that she uses to keep going and this is what she said: "Honest self-reflection helps me navigate the future."

When I think of Mikka, Matthew 10:39 comes to mind, "Whoever finds their life will lose it, and whoever loses their life for my sake will find it."

We honor Mikka today by sharing a poem written by her beloved sister. Enjoy, be encouraged and remember: YOU TOO ARE A SINGLE PARENT SUPERSTAR!

Title: ^_blue^_^_yellow^_
Written by Bobi Newsome 2/18/2012

Humble stole her glance, shy looked away
Silence whispers secrets and intention listens
Feelings spring but discipline paces her stride and asks important questions
Anticipation calls disappointment and they escape to a quaint café for tea
They hung up caution on the coat rack, and told jealousy jive jokes
While making time to make time, they learned the definition of a moment
without even knowing it
Decisive shows procrastination how to navigate the backroads expeditiously
and constant communication reprogrammed vulnerability
Small hands cuddle the warm cup of tea, and they play footsies under the table as he adds honey
Hope still believes in mo betta, so they laugh a lot while making plans to make plans for forever and ever

SPS October 2018
HIGHLIGHT Story of the Month
ANDREA JORDAN is a SINGLE PARENT SUPERSTAR!!!

Andrea is a 33-year old mother with a 16-year old son and three daughters, ages 14, 10, and 5. When I first met Andrea, she seemed quiet and humble with a dedicated protection of who she was and her kids. As I observed her over time, I realized that Andrea is filled with joy. I know she experiences the daily challenges of what is required as a single parent, but she is absolutely JOYOUS! I don't mean she is giggly all over the place by any means. She emits a quiet beauty and strength and is continually positive and hopeful, putting her trust in the Lord.

Andrea is a gifted minister of dance. Surely, her sincere, heartfelt worship must be an expression of her appreciation of the Lord, her Father. When she dances, it is personal, joyous and uplifting and anyone watching will likely join in the celebration.

Andrea's home is welcoming and she has trained her children that only teamwork will allow them to get things done as a family. I remember watching her 10-year-old cleaning up the kitchen. She washed the dishes and cleaned the countertops and everything else that was needed. I realized that I'd failed as a parent. I'm joking! Her daughter worked seamlessly. Each of her kids respect Mom and quietly fall in line with whatever they are asked. In my opinion, something beautiful and honorable has been transferred to them by Andrea.

The following is an excerpt of Andrea's SPS interview:

Monica: Andrea, do me a favor and tell me a little bit about yourself and your family.

Andrea: I am strong. We are strong together. I have encouragement in my heart. I believe in encouraging. I remember a time when I was wild and crazy and my children modeled me....they too were wild and crazy. Now, I have a clear mind. I am a leader and my children are as well. I have a lot to learn but...yeah...

Monica: Wow that is interesting. Would you please share a word of encouragement with other SPS that you use to keep going?

Andrea: There was a time in my life where I was taking everyone else's advice. I would see they were a good parent or mother and I was asking all over the place and taking everyone's advice, except God's, on how I should deal with my children. It lead me down a path of destruction. It was hell. They were good people but the advice just did not work. When I tried what I had heard from them, it split my home. As a result, there was no unity in my house. I was confused with no peace. When I asked God, He showed me how to love. He showed me how to love myself and my children through His Way, which was the right way.

Monica: That is a wonderful testimony Andrea. Please tell us what is your favorite WORD to meditate on and draw strength from?

Andrea: Trust in the Lord with all your heart and lean not on your own understanding; in all your ways submit to him, and he will make your paths straight. ***Proverbs 3:5-6***

Monica: It is amazing to ask you questions and then just listen to you share your heart. Would you please tell us one of the lessons that you have learned from your children that has impacted your life?

Andrea: I have learned forgiveness from them. They forgave me and taught me the art or power of love through forgiveness and starting anew. I understand there is power in forgiveness and I have to forgive others. I have also learned from them that it is okay to mess up and to keep going!

Monica: This is so good Andrea. Thank you for being transparent and willing to share yourself with others. YOU ARE A SINGLE PARENT SUPERSTAR!!! We are honored to highlight you this month and expect that your words will encourage others. Congratulations Andrea!

SPS July 2019
HIGHLIGHT Story of the Month
CORRYN BELLAMY is a SINGLE PARENT SUPERSTAR!!!

Corryn Bellamy is a 39-year-old young woman, born in California with roots in North Carolina but has lived in Maryland most of her life. Corryn is not only a single mother, but also a teacher in Montgomery County Public Schools and an all-around community builder.

Corryn is a giver. I've seen Corryn working major projects in service. She is also a songstress, using her voice in leading others in praise and worship of the Lord. It is clear that Corryn is a life-learner. Dedicated to the youth, providing extensions of herself to them in multiple ways. Corryn is a community builder with the ability to challenge the next generation to be the best they can be, not settling at all but reaching for the stars!

I've known Corryn and her daughter for some years now. Corryn's style is strength in a no-nonsense, unapologetic way. She has lived a little and developed a tough exterior, where if you only scratch the surface, you could miss the beauty of what is within. She is a child of God, and a student of the WORD of God who has made her personal relationship with God priority.

Watching from the sidelines, I have seen Corryn's diligence in her personal pursuit in "becoming" in the Lord, from commitment to growing in the Word of God to application of faith and being the best mother, she can be. In her local church, she is serving. In her profession, she is serving. Even as she has to work through life's challenges, she is present, engaged and serving. It is evident that her daughter has and will continue to benefit from her sacrifice for years to come.

I recently had the pleasure of interviewing Corryn. I listened to her speak from the heart about her experience as a single parent and how God has caused her to win. This is what she shared:

Monica: Corryn would you please share a word of encouragement that you use to keep going for other Single Parent Superstars?

Corryn: The short story is that I've learned how not to try and "fix it" all by myself. I was pregnant while in undergraduate school and although it took me a very long time to finish my Bachelor's degree after having a child, I did it. I was that person, on the hustle, working two and three jobs, living paycheck to paycheck, trying to make ends meet. I believed, then, that I just had to work, work, work and make it happen myself. My daughter's father was very inconsistent financially and I felt I needed to pick up the slack. I tried to do God's job. In the past that is what I did. I didn't have peace.

I have learned that I am not alone. I don't need to attempt to do things in my own strength. I'm a mom but I am God's child. I don't have to do His job.

I didn't want to stretch out higher education, so I went back to school full-time and earned my master's degree. God made a way. I worked towards getting a life for me but was not willing to ruin my daughter's life in the process. Truly, faith without work is dead. I've learned how to trust in God and not myself. Now, I have peace.

Monica: Is there any WORD in particular that has propelled you forward? Any WORD that you've used to meditate on and draw strength from?

Corryn: The enemy's goal is to make your problems seem bigger than God and that is a lie. God is not a liar. Doubt is a problem. When presented with life, bills, turmoil, desires of the heart...remember God promised peace.

1 Peter 5:7 Cast all your anxiety on Him because He cares for you.

Monica: Please share a lesson that has impacted your life.

Corryn: My daughter and I are experiencing new and wonderful things together. She will be graduating high school soon and we are very excited. She and I were talking about how fast this last year is going to go. We've been together on the grind. I'm almost 40 years of age and our lives are changing right before our eyes.

I've recently gotten engaged to be married and I remember a time where I couldn't see settling down, I felt challenged inside because I had a child. My mother was a single parent and I remember the men my mom dated. I was reluctant to date. I've always known my daughter was watching and I struggled inside knowing I needed to manage my single parent circumstance. There were also limits with time and all daily living required. I was in and out of dating, mostly out until a couple friends encouraged me to try something new.

As a single parent, I have not allowed pain, disappointment nor fear to prevent me from trying to live. God continues to lead and guide me forward. I believe we can have misplaced expectations with our children, not giving them room to be, as well as with others who become part of our lives, thinking they will be whoever we have made up in our minds.

Yes, single parenting is hard. We do our best to work through the dry spaces. God provides. He rewards our trust in Him. He is faithful and does what He says He will do.

I am engaged to be married now and my fiancé wants a family. My daughter has watched me, is aware of what I have gone through and is transitioning with me. When she realized I was serious about the person I had allowed into our lives, her initial response was not a good one. She told me she could not understand why this man was always including her and caring about her every day. She said this was "my thing". She even asked me why and how I expected her to be excited. I realized then that it was actually my fault that she felt this way. She had normalized dysfunction.

We talked and I acknowledged her pain and where it had come from. I let her know that attention and involvement in each other's daily lives is normal and welcomed. We spoke at length and worked through her feelings. Now she was in a position to deal with her feelings and change her expectations. I did my part and she was postured to move forward. She has since come around. She expressed to me recently that she is now excited about getting older and wanting to have family and kids! My experience and what she has experienced through me has affected her positively and I know that is God.

Monica: WOW!!! This is a glorious testimony Corryn! Thank you for being transparent and willing to share yourself with others. I know other SPS will be inspired by your words. YOU ARE A SINGLE PARENT SUPERSTAR! We are honored to highlight you this month and expect your words will greatly encourage others. Congratulations Corryn!

SPS July 2020
Highlight Story of the Month
PARIS THOMAS is a SINGLE PARENT SUPERSTAR!!!

Paris is a 29-year old young woman and mother with two sons. She was born in the District of Columbia and went back and forth between Suitland, Maryland and Northwest D.C., where her family had a family house. In 2013, she made the decision to attend school full time at Harmons Beauty School, earning her Cosmetology license. She is now a self-employed businesswoman, managing both Ms. Paris Does It All Hairstyling and Love of Cinn Natural Hair & Skin products. She is also a part-time stylist at another prestigious, well-known natural hair center in the DC Metro region, wanting to remain current and in the "loop", mapping her busy schedule around her sons.

Paris and I had spoken on multiple occasions and something about her screamed single parent superstar. When she agreed to be interviewed and highlighted by SPS, I expected that we'd have an opportunity to dive deeper and God would reveal something more beautiful than I could imagine. I recently had the pleasure of having lunch with Paris on a hot, summer day in July. I must say from the start that Paris looks like a ray of sunshine. Her soft speech and quiet demeanor is pleasant and welcoming, even calming. Her beauty permeates from the inside out. She has presence and I am thankful for her willingness to meet with me and share her story.

As we sat outside and broke bread together, I asked her to describe her experience as a single parent. After telling me how the COVID-19 pandemic and life adjustment had provided a break from the usual stress, she began to speak about her life experiences and how they've impacted her mothering.

Her boys are ages 7 and 9 and she describes them as vibrant and domesticated. She describes one of them as adventurous, rises early, keeps clothes on all day and is ready for whatever comes while the other is like a hermit crab, super-talented and believes that money grows on trees.

She recalled her pregnancy with her oldest son was stressful. Her relationship with this son's father (Dad A) had started from a very young age. She was only 19 when he was born with a brain injury and seizures. He remained in the hospital's Neonatal Intensive Care Unit (NICU) for two weeks after birth. From the beginning, health care professionals warned of slow development and bleak health outcomes. Paris recalls that her son was able to pass developmental benchmarks but has had ongoing daycare and now school issues as the years have progressed. She remembers having a sick child with lots of help, and Dad A just not being quite ready.

Paris then shared that the second son's father (Dad B) was a friend and seemed to have "stepped up" at a time when she definitely needed some help as she took on daily challenges presented with having a sick child. She recalled Dad B telling her that it will all be well. Shortly thereafter, she became pregnant with her second son.

She paused the story to show me a video of the youngest son singing. He had grabbed a YouTube melody and was easily belting out his own ordered lyrics. It is always amazing to see how children are so unique, born with God-given gifts and talents and with purpose, no matter the circumstance they are born into. Paris continued to share that she jumped into the new relationship with Dad B before having closure from the previous relationship with Dad A, with babies resulting from both.

Paris explained that she was getting to know Dad B and her second son at the same time.

Next, she made a comment straight from her heart. She said she felt as if she had four children now. I asked Paris what would make her posture herself as a mother of four, to include two adult males? This was her response:

> "I didn't have parents. My father was absent and my mother was hardly ever around. My grandmother did not take guardianship of me, I think, because she always hoped my mother would kind of get

it together and be there for me. Grandma had been neglected her whole life just like me and started having children at 14-years-old. I just remember being in a lot of different spaces, left alone often with other people who were not family. So much so that the people would end up calling my grandmother and saying that I had been left and needed to go home. A cousin would take me with him during summers. I remember his girlfriend whooped me once and I will never forget it. It was the first time I realized I was unprotected, and people could treat me how they wanted to. I stayed silent. I was around 5 or 6 years old then.

I learned, only recently in 2019, that my mother had been a drug addict for my whole life. I remember her telling me that I was so "green". I often wonder how I didn't know about her life-long addiction, but there was likely some brainwashing and/or denial there.

There was a time when my mom was somewhat present. She'd married a man that I thought was wonderful. My stepdad was a wonderful man and for two years, I experienced what it was like to have a strong male presence that was positive. He was a drug dealer and was killed when I was 14-years-old. I was devastated. So again, I am left with my mom. She has told me she didn't know what to do after he died. She was a diva like woman who shopped in Neiman Marcus. She had lots of struggles and would come home differently each night. One day she would come home stabbed. Another day, she would come home pregnant and in need of an abortion. Often times, she would come home drugged out. I thought it was normal for a long time, but my heart felt it wasn't.

I always gave my mother respect though. I recall her telling me that I needed to always listen to and obey her. Even though I saw her living like she did, I never disrespected her. I still obeyed and loved her."

I chimed in here because Ephesians 6 came to mind. "***Children, obey your parents the way the Lord wants, because this is the right thing to do. 2 The command says, "You must respect your father and mother." This is the first command that has a promise with it. 3 And this is the promise*: "*Then all will go well with you, and you will have a long life on the earth*."

Paris and I discussed how even in imperfections; God can use people to impart life giving truth.

Paris continued, "I went through a lot of things alone. I remember mom signing me up for dance. She didn't stay around to make sure I got to class or had what I needed for class or made sure that class actually happened. She just disappeared. Grandma was there for me and Aunt Doll was good to me too. Aunt Doll and my uncle rented rooms out to men in the family house. That happened before I was born. I could never seem to sleep in the family house, even when I was very young. There were unclean spirits in that house and I could not rest there.

Aunt Doll always made sure I ate. My aunt and grandmother made sure I stayed alive, even though they struggled themselves. My Aunt Doll got sick and passed. Now that I am an adult, I understand everything my grandmother went through. I know it was a lot. She is a survivor and if I could write her book, I would. I love my mom and she is still a young woman, and I will always support her within reason. I signed her up for a drug treatment program once. She declined and I gave it to God."

I interrupted Paris here because I could see that she is not only a survivor but also takes it upon herself to parent everyone around her, mostly adults. It was clear that she has had to do this all of her life. I encouraged her to try and focus on herself and her children with no guilt. Her time and effort spread out to other adults continually can be draining and takes away from her own healthy growth and development. We all need Jesus and sometimes people make us their God or we want other people to be our God and meet all of our needs. Only God can do that.

Only God can be God. Attention to our personal relationship with the Lord, Jesus frees us up and is satisfying. Paris responded in letting me know that she has been working on re-directing and that while it takes time, the process had definitely started.

Paris continued, "...I remember mom asking me why I wanted a family so soon. Well, I never had a family. I have not, even up until this day, had a chance to talk to my biological father. I did speak with his dad, my grandfather. I confronted him and let him know that I remembered him opting out of this relationship. I told him how no one else is here and thinking about him like me. He looked at me and said, 'Paris, I just had to turn that over to God'."

As Paris spoke, I listened and realized that Paris could easily have been dead in every sense of the word; physically, emotionally, and spiritually dead. She had experienced a series of traumas, one on top of another. But Paris is not dead. She is alive and walking in God's Healing!

Another scripture that came to mind that I shared with her is ***Psalm 27:10 When my father and mother abandon me, the Lord will take me up***.

We discussed how she was an overcomer and how God is always there, especially in our times of need. We talked about how God delivers us out of difficulty time and time again. I shared with Paris examples of God helping me when no one else would or could. When I shared with her how God came to me after my husband died and told me He was the Lord my God who takes me by my right hand and says do not fear, I will help you (Isaiah 41:13), she began to cry. I cried too because when we are weak, He is strong.

I asked Paris what she is thankful for today? Paris responded by saying she is trying to give her boys experiences that she never had; consistency that she never had. She said she was building a foundation. She commented that if they have struggles it won't be because mom was causing it. She said she was committed to not having her oldest son being left to raise his younger brother. She wants them to go places and see things that she was never able to see, to travel [the world]. She is teaching them to work hard. She described in her life how she would have things for a moment, but they would be taken away, good things like her stepdad and Aunt Doll. She explained that her boys will not have experiences like she had to endure.

I told Paris she sounded hopeful. Somehow, after all she has been through, she seems to have hope and a peace about her. Jeremiah 29:11 comes to mind, "***The Lord says He knows the plans He has for us. Plans to prosper us and not to harm us. Plans of hope and a future.***" It is amazing to me how even in a desert, the Lord, Jesus quenches our thirst. He is a well of living water that never runs dry and makes the impossible possible for those who believe.

Paris went on to explain how she is thankful for her children and how they simplify things. She feels God gave her two men. One of them always says emphatically to her that he loves God. She says her children are a daily reminder that things don't have to be bad all of the time. I reminded Paris that trusting in the Lord and having faith was not automatic. While we have a measure of faith, it must be built on. ***Faith comes by hearing and hearing by the Word of God - Romans 10:17***.

Paris and I spoke for a few hours and it was a blessing for us both, especially me! There is no way to capture all of the goodness that came out of our time together. I asked her if she would kindly share a word of encouragement that she uses to keep going to help other Single Parent Superstars.

She quoted rapper Kevin Gates, "No matter the circumstance, whatever you do, is part of your character."

Paris is about positive energy and wishes for us to admonish one another by repeating this call and response:

"Respect yourself. Respect yourself also."

She yearns for peaceful unity, not only in her family, but also in her community.

Congratulation Paris! God loves you! You are royalty and deserve the best God has to offer!

YOU ARE A SINGLE PARENT SUPERSTAR!

SPS April 2022
Highlight Story of the Month
VANETTE BLOUNT is a SINGLE PARENT SUPERSTAR!!!

First off, this is an amazing story. Vanette's testimony is truly inspiring, and I am truly honored to highlight her as the spotlight story this April 2022. Let me start by making a confession. Vanette and I have been friends for over 27 years. When my friend gave birth to her beautiful baby girl and she was not walking by the age of two, I attempted to analyze what I thought I saw. In my defense, I was a young science major in college, and in my mind, I was helping my friend settle in practical observation. Was my friend in denial? Was my friend choosing avoidance? Was she just not able to cope with what was before her? I, sort of, remember looking up different diseases and trying to diagnose a disability. I must tell this story, and I am so thankful and pleased Vanette has agreed to allow it to be told. Not for one second did Vanette verbalize a disease or diagnose Tyler as having a disability. She never, ever did that. She resisted my words from the very beginning and responded in FAITH. Faith is the substance of things hoped for and the evidence of things unseen (Hebrews 11:1 KJV). Another way to say it is...faith is what makes real the things we hope for. It is proof of what we cannot see. (Hebrews 11:1 ERV). Vanette called her daughter what God said, not what I said, or what the world said. Moreover, today, as Tyler is a grown, beautiful, intelligent, funny woman, she is a walking miracle. Tyler has flourished and I have watched Vanette set and maintain a very high bar in standard of living practice. Because of this action, because of faith, Tyler lives up to the challenge and thrives.

During the interview, Vanette reminded me of a day when we were at King's Dominion, trying to park, so we could go into the amusement park. Crystal, who Vanette describes as the mom of our friend group, suggested Vanette get a motor vehicle handicap tag, "so that when you and Tyler go places you can use handicap parking privileges". Vanette's stance was no, we want Tyler's legs strengthened and no she is not handicapped. Vanette recalled, on another day, watching television and seeing a Melwood commercial, offering services for those having disabilities. There was a phrase Vanette heard and wrote on her heart immediately. Persons were described as having "DIFFERING ABILITIES", not disabilities. Vanette shared how she only saw that commercial once. After that day, she never saw it again. In one moment, she got a word and wrote it on her heart for a lifetime.

Vanette says to really trust God, to be a follower of the Lord Jesus Christ, you almost have to be crazy. We are in this world but not of this world (ref. John 17:14-16). People will think you are crazy. Vanette says, "Now, I preface myself with people...I am crazy. I have crazy faith. I have faith in God. Tyler's way of maneuvering is different from others. It is not a disability. If you want to call it a disability, what is yours? Something is bound to happen in your life that will require you to talk different, walk different and live different. You will be different from your family, from your friends and co-workers. They will think you are crazy."

Vanette shared that she believed God would make a way for her to help other parents. If parents do not have a spiritual foundation, they will believe what the world says, and their children will likely fall into believing what the world says. "Tyler has physical challenges but what about people with emotional, learning or behavioral challenges?" Vanette commented that God made us individual. "How are you going to put a label on me because my issue is different from yours or I am different from you? When it comes to education and life in general, children need an advocate!"

Vanette shared a story with me that happened before she became a mom. It happened with a regular customer at a pharmacy counter, an Indian woman, who frequented the store she worked at. The woman was not a pastor, deacon or anyone with a title. She was just a woman who spoke to Vanette one day, asking her if she had a Bible. She asked Vanette if she had read the Bible. Vanette responded with yes, two or three times.

The woman then asked Vanette "Well, what have you gotten from reading it?"

Vanette said, "It helped me to know how much God loves me."

The woman said to her, "Do you know that when someone loves you, they want to give you things? When you read the Bible, you are supposed to be looking for the promises of God. You look for them, so you know what you are entitled to."

The woman told Vanette, "Highlight every promise in the Bible, so that when you go back again, you could find them easily, without too much trouble. Imagine each promise as a present with a bow on it."

Vanette went on to share she does not know when she will see Tyler's full healing manifestation with her physical eyes but she knows it is already done. "Tyler walking is done. I fully expect to see Tyler walking down the aisle on her wedding day."

Vanette: "All I know is that right before she was born, I had taken some time off, in an attempt to use up some vacation leave. I went to the grocery store that day. I remember feeling tired, while walking down [the] grocery aisles. I got home, ate something and laid down on the couch. I went to bed earlier than usual and by the middle of the night, I had pain. It was not excruciating pain, just discomfort. The feeling of needing to urinate had gotten more frequent so I called the OBGYN. The doctor said, 'I needed to be checked out' and instructed me to 'go to the hospital'. However, when babies are going to come, they are coming. They follow God's order. Planning does not mean anything! The baby is coming according to God's plan. I remember trying to get up off the toilet and realizing I was not making it to any hospital. I said, Lord help me. Help me now. Most of my life I had had irregular cycles. I never really believed I could get pregnant. I was 34 years old, having had a string of bad relationships and bad choices. Again, I did not think I would ever be pregnant. I did not realize my pregnancy until 3-4 months in. I remember I could not start my day without reading my Bible. People call it prayer. I just call it conversation. I do not even know if I know how to pray. However, I do know that if you go to Him with a sincere heart, He hears you. I know how to talk to God. I know how to praise God. He is great and He is mighty. I know how to talk to God. God knows I do not necessarily like this person (Tyler's Father) but I love him because of the beautiful child we made together. I know God wants me to be kind, so that is what I am going to do. I will do that until God makes me better, until I am different."

Monica: "What do you see when you look at Tyler today?"

Vanette: "Tyler, herself, has given her life to Christ. Some parents believe it is because of them. I am not that stupid. In my attempt to be a better me, a good mother, I was able to help her be drawn to God. I like who my daughter is, who she is becoming as a woman. The person she is is a blessing. I like that person. The world does not stop. I do not want people stopping her world. I want her to matriculate into the world in her own way. Stop for her because she is gorgeous. Stop for her because you heard her beautiful laugh. Do not stop because her way of maneuvering is different from yours or because she had "differing abilities". Do not stop her world!

I have been blessed and favored to see angels. God has been kind to me, and He sent angels for me. I remember running late one morning, going to church. My brother, Vincent, had driven that day, and was far ahead, because he walks fast. We walked past this McDonald's and this older woman appeared. I know she was not there before. She was standing there at the fast-food restaurant, near the sidewalk by a tree. She said to me, 'Good morning, you got a lovely baby. You know God says everything is alright'. I said yes. The woman said, 'No! I'm saying that God says it really is alright.' I did turn around, after I passed, and that woman was no longer there. With all of the blessings, favor and miracles that Tyler and I have already experienced, I know from reading the same Bible, with the same highlighted promises, there are many, many more of these things to come.

Monica: "Please share an encouraging word for single parents or any parent with a child with "differing abilities" and include a scripture that is a go to for you."

Vanette: "Let your children know we are all fearfully and wonderfully made.

For you created my inmost being; you knit me together in my mother's womb. I praise you because I am fearfully and wonderfully made; your works are wonderful; I know that full well. (Psalm 139:13-14 NIV)

We have to know whose we are, not who the child is or who the child's earthly parents are. It is important to establish identity (in Christ) early on. God himself took the time to make sure each and every human being is different and cannot be duplicated. If each and every one of us has a unique fingerprint, that is distinctive, how awesome is it that we are so unique. I am a jewel, a treasure, a one-of-a-kind masterpiece. I have to be a gift to the world. I can never be you and you can never be me. Tell your children the truth. They belong to God!"

Monica: "Whew! Glory to God! That is awesome friend. YOU ARE A SINGLE PARENT SUPERSTAR! Your words will help many parents to speak life to their children. Congratulations Vanette! You and Tyler are amazing women of God and living proof of the miraculous.

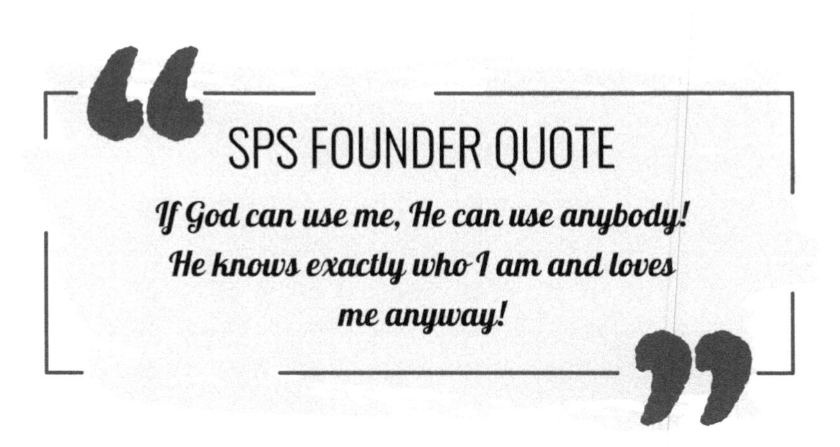

Dear SPS Letter 6:

PREVENTATIVE MEASURES

Dear Single-Parent Superstar,

In the time that I have engaged the single parent community, I have made this observation: there are single parents who feel as if they have raised kids and have, to some degree, **"been there, done that"** and are not the **"target population"** for what the Single Parent Superstars organization offers. On some level, I can understand this stance. However, I believe it is necessary to shine a light on or acknowledge the fact that preventative measures are rooted in the SPS principles and misconceptions. I do not think there is one person in the world who could honestly say raising a child alone is easy. We have discussed how single parents are not only young teenage girls but also young teenage boys, grown women/men, divorcees or widows/widowers. Each of these groups are likely people who have ended up in a situation that they did not plan to be their reality. Some people do plan single parenthood, but that is another letter altogether. (Sigh)

When I have experienced a situation that is perpetually difficult for me and even more so for my child, the last thing I want to see is one of my children, coming of age and walking down the same path! I do not want to see my children and cousins becoming single parents. I do not want to see my neighbors becoming single parents. I do not want to see strangers suffering either! I do not wish single parenthood on anyone because what it requires, on a daily basis, is almost indescribable, even though a wonderful gift from God is wrapped up in it. We cannot be so arrogant and think ***I already know that*** and then watch as loved ones who are in arms reach, that we have access to and some level of influence on, walk into the very same situations. Single parenthood is not an inevitable or inescapable status quo. Knowledge is power! Sharing information, even as support of PREVENTION, is love. I know that we cannot control others, but we can support them in prevention. I would rather be informed and still get myself into a sticky situation, than to be ignorant with no clue and get myself into a sticky situation. The former of the two is better!

Now I declare, in Jesus Name, that I AM A SINGLE PARENT SUPERSTAR and that YOU ARE A SINGLE PARENT SUPERSTAR!! I will not romanticize the single parent position at all. If I have never said it before, please avoid becoming a single parent!

Single Parent Superstars are parents who do their very best every day to positively affect their kids. Single Parent Superstars work with purpose, always putting their children first. The SPS organization acts as a community of parents who through mentoring, advocacy and support, strive to overcome the difficulties of life for ourselves and for the benefit of our children AND PREVENTION IS ROOTED IN OUR CAUSE!

Please do not reject being open to knowledge and power and sharing it...or getting a different messenger to share God-given wisdom. Sometimes good information coming from others, who are not so close, settles easier. We must remain teachable as we are here for one another and will affect generations to come.

Much Love and Respect,

Monica

ONLY YOU KNOW YOUR STORY

So now, you have finished the book. You have read some things about me (that I would have loved to keep secret) and about others. I pray you were encouraged. I pray you received mentorship, felt advocated for and supported. I hope you laughed. Sometimes we have to laugh to keep from crying. The Bible says, "laughter is medicine to our bones." I hope this reading experience added to your identity. If you were not saved before picking up this book, I pray you have received Christ and became a child of God by the time you finish this book. If you were already a believer, I hope your faith and expectation increased exponentially. In case you got to the end and felt like you could not relate to anything I shared or that your single parent experience is nothing like mine nor anyone else in this book, I challenge you to go deeper. Your story is definitely not my story, but if you are a single parent, you have a story. What is the Lord saying to you? God is the same yesterday, today and forever. He does not play favorites. Both, you and I are His favorite child. If you didn't know this already, I pray your personal relationship with the Lord be strengthened and that you come to realize you are His favorite child too.

YOU ARE A SINGLE PARANT SUPERSTAR! Because of your sacrifice, your children will walk out their purposes in life. Because of your effort, your children will overcome disappointments, depression, pain and suffering. Because of you, your children will have access to positive growth and development that is beneficial for generations to come. Because of you, your children will shine bright like stars in night sky and they will be blessings to others. The spirit of the living God is on the inside of you, causing you and yours to prosper. Be encouraged, you are not alone. God loves our children more than you or I ever could.

THE GOOD NEWS

Everyone can use "The Good News"

For God so loved the world that He sent His only Son that whoever believes in Him, shall not perish but have eternal life. (John 3:16)

The good news is Jesus died for the whole world, all mankind. Not one person is left out of this equation. When He died, He took away sin, shame, and death. When we accept Him as Savior and Lord, and ask Him to come into our hearts, we have a spiritual re-birth, instantly. All mankind must be born again. A decision for Jesus Christ is eternal. Salvation is a free gift that none of us can earn. Wrapped in salvation is healing, deliverance and freedom that only God provides, even as we live in this dirty, rotten world. This is NOT a religion. There are thousands of religions based on groups and separation. This is a personal relationship with God through the Lord, Jesus Christ.

Rejecting the free gift of salvation is choosing to be responsible for sin. Jesus has already died for the sins of the whole world. Do not choose to be responsible for sin when God has already responded for us. Jesus paid the price already, for while we were yet sinners, Christ died for us**.** **(ref. Romans 5:8)**

This is good news for everyone, including you and me.

The world has many limits, but there are no limits in Christ Jesus. God calls us Single Parent Superstars and gives us the strength to be the best that we can be. Because of Him, the impossible is possible. It is up to us to believe and receive and expect that He will do exactly what He promises. Remember, and make this declaration by faith:

YOU ARE A SINGLE PARENT SUPERSTAR!!!